OECD Public Governance Reviews

Internal Audit Manual for the Greek Public Administration

This work is published under the responsibility of the Secretary-General of the OECD. The opinions expressed and arguments employed herein do not necessarily reflect the official views of OECD member countries.

This document, as well as any data and any map included herein, are without prejudice to the status of or sovereignty over any territory, to the delimitation of international frontiers and boundaries and to the name of any territory, city or area.

Please cite this publication as:
OECD (2018), *Internal Audit Manual for the Greek Public Administration*, OECD Public Governance Reviews, OECD Publishing, Paris.
https://doi.org/10.1787/9789264309692-en

ISBN 978-92-64-30968-5 (print)
ISBN 978-92-64-30969-2 (pdf)

Series: OECD Public Governance Reviews
ISSN 2219-0406 (print)
ISSN 2219-0414 (online)

The statistical data for Israel are supplied by and under the responsibility of the relevant Israeli authorities. The use of such data by the OECD is without prejudice to the status of the Golan Heights, East Jerusalem and Israeli settlements in the West Bank under the terms of international law.

Photo credits: Cover © Mantopoulos Marie

Corrigenda to OECD publications may be found on line at: *www.oecd.org/publishing/corrigenda*.

© OECD 2018

You can copy, download or print OECD content for your own use, and you can include excerpts from OECD publications, databases and multimedia products in your own documents, presentations, blogs, websites and teaching materials, provided that suitable acknowledgement of OECD as source and copyright owner is given. All requests for public or commercial use and translation rights should be submitted to *rights@oecd.org*. Requests for permission to photocopy portions of this material for public or commercial use shall be addressed directly to the Copyright Clearance Center (CCC) at *info@copyright.com* or the Centre français d'exploitation du droit de copie (CFC) at *contact@cfcopies.com*.

Foreword

Since the economic crisis, Greece has made substantial progress in implementing public governance and fiscal reforms. The government's National Strategy for Administrative Reform 2017 - 2020, outlines the structural initiatives for an independent, meritocratic and effective public administration to help address the root causes of the financial crisis. Within this framework, a highly capable and efficient internal audit function is essential for holding the public sector accountable and restoring trust in government institutions.

The approach to internal control and audit in the Greek public administration is largely legalistic and compliance-oriented. Yet, internal audit's primary goal is to assure government and citizens that appropriate and cost-effective controls are in place across public organisations. Internal audit is a champion of value-for-money for taxpayers while holding the government accountable for its performance. The internal audit function, as highlighted in the Greek National Anti-Corruption Plan (NACAP), also plays a vital role in preventing and detecting corruption.

In line with the NACAP's objectives, this Internal Audit Manual supports audit entities in modernising their practices and strengthening their capacity. Moreover, it can serve as an insightful practical guide and benefit other public administrations undergoing similar reforms. The Manual is part of a comprehensive package of innovative guides and practical tools, which was developed by the OECD and encompasses all the elements necessary for a sound internal audit function. It goes beyond reviewing the existing institutional control and audit framework by proposing concrete measures to address identified weaknesses, based on international standards and good practices.

In addition to this manual, the package includes a step-by-step guide on how to undertake a core control audit, a training programme for internal auditors, and a needs assessment for an e-platform to support audit work. The tools provided are meant to support Greek authorities in their efforts to develop a more effective and efficient internal audit function. The OECD developed this work in close co-operation with various national stakeholders, such as the General Secretariat against Corruption and audit authorities, and it benefitted from the valuable insights of international experts.

This Internal Audit Manual was prepared by the Public Sector Integrity Division of the OECD Directorate for Public Governance as part of the Greece-OECD Project on Technical Support for Anti-Corruption. The work was led by Angelos Binis and Terry Hunt with guidance from Julio Bacio Terracino. Pelagia Patsoule and Katerina Kanellou provided insights and facilitated meetings and workshops with Greek stakeholders. Laura McDonald managed communications and editing. The text was edited by Julie Harris and Meral Gedik, while Alpha Zambou provided essential administrative support.

This document was produced with the financial assistance of the European Union. The views expressed herein can in no way be taken to reflect the official opinion of the European Union.

Table of contents

Tables

Figures

Boxes

Follow OECD Publications on:

http://twitter.com/OECD_Pubs

http://www.facebook.com/OECDPublications

http://www.linkedin.com/groups/OECD-Publications-4645871

http://www.youtube.com/oecdilibrary

http://www.oecd.org/oecddirect/

Executive summary

This Internal Audit Manual is designed to assist Greece's public sector audit entities in building their professional capacity. It proposes a solid framework for an effective internal audit function, and offers practical guidance on standardising and modernising audit practices across the public sector. It provides tools to help internal audit units (IAUs) plan and undertake effective internal audit missions, prepare risk-based audit plans (RBAPs) and conduct fraud risk assessments.

As is the case with many countries, Greece is currently modernising its control system to reinforce the accountability of its public institutions. Modern internal control frameworks require each public institution to administer its own internal control programme and are based on the premise that public institutions are required to assemble sound management and financial control arrangements. Embedded in an institution's systems and processes, as a system of checks and balances, internal controls must be performed across all governance and operational arrangements. Equipping each line ministry with tools and capacities for a strong and independent internal audit function is thus critical for an effective internal control system.

This Internal Audit Manual responds to five questions at the heart of the work of the internal audit units of the Greek central public administration:

- How to build an effective audit function?
- How to develop a risk-based audit plan?
- How to help entities and programmes become "audit ready"?
- How to undertake a fraud risk assessment?
- How to undertake an audit engagement from start to finish?

It also offers a series of tools, such as a competencies framework and job descriptions for internal auditors, fraud risk assessment guidance and tools, and risk-based audit planning tools. The Manual also presents methods for promoting audit independence, including detailed guidelines for developing audit charters and introducing a new concept within Greece, the ministerial audit committees.

Reinforcing the internal audit function is a key aspect of Greece's anti-corruption efforts. This Manual contributes to achieving the goals of the National Anti-Corruption Plan regarding the modernisation of the internal audit function and strengthening the capacity of internal audit entities. The Manual is tailored to the specific characteristics of the Greek national context and institutional framework. However, the insights and lessons it contains can be used by any public administration seeking to strengthen its internal control system and enhancing its internal audit capacity.

1. Introduction

1.1. Purpose

The purpose of this Audit Manual is to help standardise and modernise audit practices across all ministries within the Greek public service that possess internal audit functions and help establish one where needed. It also aims to provide hands-on tools to help conduct effective internal audits.

1.2. Background

The General Secretariat Against Corruption (GSAC), Ministry of Justice, Transparency and Human Rights; the Structural Reform Support Service (SRSS), European Commission; and, the Organisation for Economic Co-operation and Development (OECD) are key stakeholders in the Greece-OECD Technical Support Project on Anti-Corruption. The project spans 18 months and addresses 10 components. This manual pertains to the first component that focuses on strengthening internal control and audit for increased accountability and good governance.

Contemporary internal control holds all public institutions accountable. It requires each public institution to administer its own internal control programme and is based on the premise that each institution ought to manage its finances in delivering outputs. Thus, public institutions are required to assemble a financial control department, i.e., put in place a comptrollership function.

> The public administration in Greece is in the process of modernising its control framework. Within such a model, implementing a modern approach to internal audit becomes increasingly important.

Contemporary internal controls are embedded in an entity's managerial processes as checks and balances performed at all layers. Norms and values are internalised rather than being imposed externally. More emphasis is given to horizontal and hierarchical interactions within the institution. Contemporary internal control, therefore, assigns responsibilities to all staff and not only to the budget and accounting officials.

However, the success of an internal control system is profoundly affected not only by the attitudes of the management and employees, but also by the establishment of safeguards. The following features of a management system for internal controls are important to efficacy: 1) decisive leadership that is responsible for designing, implementing, supervising, maintaining, and documenting the internal control system; 2) well-considered internal control design aligned with organisational objectives; 3) committed personnel who perform their jobs in accordance with the pre-stated policies, procedures, regulations, and ethical rules; 4) effective risk identification and system monitoring mechanisms; and 5) internal audit and independent internal auditors are part of an internal control system that provides a set of sound safeguarding processes.[1]

1.3. Methodology

This Audit Manual is geared to the Greek central public administration. It was prepared on the basis of substantial consultations, interviews, focus groups, and a two-day consultation workshop.

Meetings were held between 20 October and 10 November 2016 with 26 governmental organisations and 3 non-governmental organisations; they involved 60 individuals. The two-day consultation workshop with over 145 audit community members was undertaken on 5 and 6 December 2016. Throughout these consultations, participants were asked to identify what the Audit Manual should address and what hands-on tools should be included.

Several Greek ministry audit manuals and documents were reviewed, as well as a number of international audit manuals. In addition, a legislation and literature review was undertaken.

This Audit Manual should be read in conjunction with the OECD Technical Report on Mapping and Gap Analysis of the Greek Public Administration, and the Core Control Audit Programme, published separately. In order to avoid duplication, the topics addressed in these reports, such as an overview of the Greek audit community and differences between internal and external audit, internal control, and investigations, are not addressed in this manual.

1.4. What is internal audit?

The terminology of this manual uses international standards established by the Institute of Internal Auditors' (IIA) International Professional Practices Framework (IPPF).

Internal audit is a professional, independent appraisal function that provides feedback on government management practices and activities at the ministry/agency level. The function assists in promoting the overall effectiveness and efficiency of government operations and the transparency of decision making.

Internal audit provides senior management and elected officials with assurance as to the design and operation of the governance, risk management, and control processes in their organisations. This assurance function is an important part of the government's efforts to provide value and accountability to Greek citizens for their tax contributions.

The focus of internal audit is on management systems, processes and practices, and on the integrity of financial and non-financial information. The results of internal audits help to identify emerging issues and make recommendations for the improvement of performance.

Figure 1.1. Internal audit

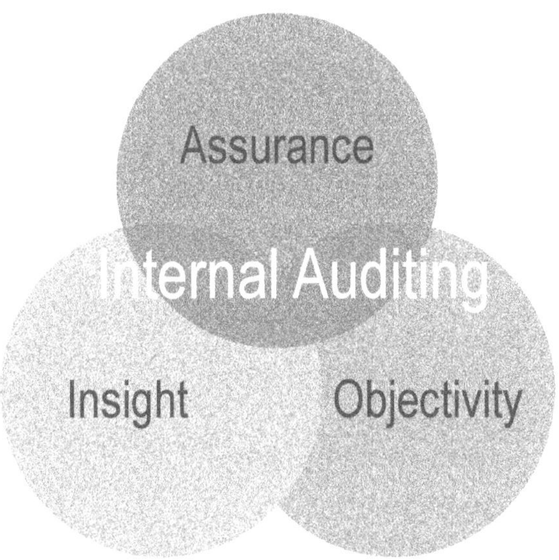

Internal auditing = assurance, insight, and objectivity

Governing bodies and senior management rely on internal auditing for objective assurance and insight on the effectiveness and efficiency of governance, risk management, and internal control processes.

Source: IIA (2015), International Professional Practices Framework, Institute of Internal Auditors.

Note

[1] World Bank (2006), *Keeping an Eye on Subnational Governments: Internal Control and Audit at Local Levels*, Mustafa Baltaci and Serdar Yilmaz Copyright, the International Bank for Reconstruction and Development/The World Bank, Washington, DC. p.11.

2. Building an effective internal audit unit

Consultations with ministries' internal audit units underlined the need for the Audit Manual to address the key steps of how to establish and mature an internal audit function.

Figure 2.1. Internal audit maturity model

Source: Adapted from IIA (2009), IPPF Supplemental Guidance: Internal Audit Capability Model (IA-CM), Institute of Internal Auditors and IIA (2012), IIPF Supplemental Guidance: Implementing a New Internal Audit Function in the Public Sector, Institute of Internal Auditors.

This section examines six key areas that the head of an internal audit function, i.e. a chief audit executive (CAE), needs to take into account when establishing an internal audit unit.[1] Some of these areas regard how internal audit function is directed; whereas others regard how internal audit is situated in the organisation. These areas include: services and role of internal audit, people management, professional practices, governance structures, organisational relationships and culture, performance management and accountability.

Box 2.1. Getting started: Key initial steps for establishing an internal audit function

The first year is essentially a test period, with the head of the audit function "selling" the need and role of internal audit while creating the necessary audit capacity to begin producing value to the organisation. These 21 steps should help organisations begin their internal audit work:

1. Establish a relationship with the legal advisor within your organisation and understand the legal basis for the creation of the internal audit function, its scope, responsibilities and authorities.
2. Open lines of communication with the head of the organisation and establish an on-going meeting schedule with him, as well as open lines of communication with the General Secretariat Against Corruption
3. Establish relationships with all senior managers within the ministry and participate as a member of the organisation's executive committee.
4. Understand and begin implementing IIA auditing standards and begin planning the future of the internal audit function.
5. Familiarise yourself with the internal control framework of your organisation, as well as established management control frameworks, such as the Committee of Sponsoring Organizations of the Treadway Commission (COSO), and the Public Internal Control (PIC), which are used by many other European Union (EU) member countries.
6. Join the IIA in order to access ongoing resources, link to the broader audit community, and access professional development resources.
7. Consider your resource needs and make a business case for an appropriately resourced internal audit function.
8. Appoint people with the right skills and experience to work in the internal audit units.
9. Interview senior managers to learn what they expect from an internal audit function and begin defining the audit universe.
10. Promote the use of control self-assessments throughout the organisation to create a pro-audit culture, enable audit entities to become "audit ready", and assist in the development of the audit universe, risk assessment, and the identification of audit priorities. This activity should include: training management on control self-assessment, and assisting in the identification of improvements to enable the organisation to become audit ready. This will also enable the audit team to learn the processes being used, evaluate internal controls, and identify common themes of concern.
11. Educate senior managers about the role and methods of internal audits, standards, and different types of audits, internal controls, etc.
12. Write the audit charter and get approval from management. Develop a mission, vision, core values and a strategic plan. Propose the need for an audit committee to help deliver IA services.
13. Conduct a risk assessment, including prioritising risks and identifying those that

can be addressed quickly to establish the benefit of an internal audit function. Determine the organisation's risk appetite.

14. Develop a draft audit plan based upon the initial risk assessment. At a minimum, it should be co-ordinated with external auditors to avoid duplication of effort.
15. Begin to conduct internal audits and implement the audit plan, recognising that senior management may require a faster implementation schedule.
16. Begin establishing a quality assurance improvement plan (QAIP). This should be an ongoing, continuous activity.
17. Identify training needs and individual learning plans of employees based upon a skills assessment and promote their certified internal auditor (CIA) and similar professional accreditations.
18. Establish ongoing outreach, input, and communication between the internal audit function and ministry managers and employees, including the continuous, ongoing marketing of internal audit. This should include developing communication tools that describe the role of internal audit and the basic audit findings while respecting the rules of "open government" and data protection.
19. Establish a performance reporting framework, (including the creation of a database to track the status of implementing the audit plan and corrective actions) to heighten internal audit's presence and communicate its value-added to the achievement of organisational objectives.
20. Establish relationships with external auditors to promote the efficient delivery of independent assurance services within the organisation.
21. Establish relationships with the broader audit community to promote continuous improvement and innovative thinking.

Source: Adapted from IIA Manual on Building IA Functions.

2.1. Services and role of internal audit

Internal audit's mission is to enhance and protect organisational value by providing risk-based and objective assurance, advice, and insight. It helps an organisation accomplish its objectives by bringing a systematic, disciplined approach to evaluate and improve the effectiveness of risk management, control, and governance processes.

However, how this role is accomplished varies among different environments. The services provided by internal audit are typically based on the organisation's needs and the internal audit unit's authority, scope, and capacity.

IIA Standard 1000: Purpose, authority, and responsibility

"The purpose, authority, and responsibility of the internal audit activity must be formally defined in an internal audit charter, consistent with the IIA Definition of Internal Auditing, the Code of Ethics, and the Standards. The chief audit executive must periodically review the internal audit charter and present it to senior management and the board for approval."

Services include the provision of assurance and consulting/advisory activities; and can consist of audits of compliance, systems, processes, operations, performance/value-for-money, information and related technology, and financial statements and systems.

The broadest audit focus considers the organisation's governance activities, which can help the organisation achieve its objectives and priority goals and improve its governance framework, including its ethical code. The narrowest audit focus involves testing individual transactions for errors or for compliance with contract terms, policies, regulations, or laws. The auditors' scope of work can vary between these extremes and includes activities such as reviewing internal controls, processes, and systems to identify systemic weaknesses and propose operational improvements.

Following IIA international standards, audit services can be broken down into three general areas as described in Figure 2.2 below. The first is the traditional assurance focus of compliance auditing, i.e. carrying out an audit of conformity and the adherence of a particular area, process, or system to policies, plans, procedures, laws, regulations, contracts, or other requirements that govern the conduct of the area, process, or system subject to audit. Outputs include documented audit engagement reports that provide guidance or advice to management, and working papers that support audit conclusions. Outcomes include: influencing change to improve the organisation's operations and adding value to the organisation by management acting on audit results; assurance that the area, process, or system subject to audit operates in compliance with relevant authorities/criteria; prevention or detection of illegal acts or violations of established policies, procedures, or contract requirements.

Figure 2.2. Types of internal audit services

Traditional assurance	Performance and assurance	Consulting services

• To carry out an audit of conformity and adherence of particular area, process, or system to policies, plans, procedures, laws, regulations, contracts, or other requirements that govern the conduct of the area, process, or system subject to audit. • Conducts sufficient work to provide an opinion on the overall adequacy and effectiveness of the organisation's governance, risk management, and control processes.	• To assess and report on the efficiency, effectiveness, and economy of operations, activities, or programs; or conduct engagements on governance, risk management, and control. Performance/value-for-money auditing covers the full spectrum of operating and business processes, the associated management controls, and the results achieved.	• Advisory Services directed toward facilitation rather than assurance and include training, systems development reviews, performance and control self-assessment, counseling, and advice. Key deliverable include: control self-assessments; assistance in developing Internal control Frameworks; and management oriented reviews.

Source: IIA international Standards: IIA (2016), International standards for the professional practice of internal auditing (standards), Institute of Internal Auditors.

Performance/value-for-money audits are a second area of activity that involve assessing and reporting on the efficiency, effectiveness, and economy of operations, activities, or programmes. They also involve audit engagements regarding governance, risk management, and control. Performance/value-for-money auditing covers the full spectrum of operating and business processes, the associated management controls, and the results achieved. Outcomes include added value by identifying opportunities to improve the achievement of organisational objectives and the improvement of the effectiveness of operations. Influencing change can contribute to and maintain more efficient, effective, and high-performing government operations.

The third area is advisory services, which analyse a situation and/or provide guidance and advice to management.[8] Advisory services add value without the internal auditor assuming management responsibility. They are directed towards facilitation rather than assurance and include training, systems development reviews, performance and control self-assessment, counselling, and advice.

Advisory services offered by an internal audit function can focus on helping management ensure that organisational services and programmes are audit ready though activities such as undertaking audit readiness reviews. This involves identifying areas that would need to be put in place in order for a programme or service to benefit from an audit. For example, providing advice on a control framework and how one is developed is much more useful than doing an audit of a programme that does not have a control framework, since that would be a starting recommendation. Thus, in the context of advisory services, internal audit enters into a partnership approach with management. Once the organisation is mature, then more aggressive conformance auditing and performance auditing could be undertaken.

When deciding what type of audit service(s) to provide, the needs of management, as well as the capacity of the audit function itself, need to be considered. Once decided upon, the type of audit service should be identified in the organisation's official audit charter.

2.2. People management

People management is the process of creating a working environment that enables people to perform to the best of their abilities. It begins when a job is defined as needed and includes building effective teams to guide improvement and progress with a training and development plan.

Figure 2.3 below presents the five core components of a sound people management framework for an internal audit function. It starts with identifying the scope of the audit function's business and the necessary human resources required to fulfil this mission. It involves having a sound organisational design of how these resources will be organised, which is supported by a concrete competency profile and associated job descriptions. Finally, learning and professional development and performance management are key to inspiring and maintaining performance.

Figure 2.3. Internal audit people management framework

Source: Adapted from: IIPF Supplemental Guidance: Implementing a New Internal Audit Function in the Public Sector, Institute of Internal Auditors.

2.2.1. Business and human resources planning

A key role of the chief audit executive is to identify resource needs and make a business case to senior management about why investing in internal audit is a value-added, strategic investment on the part of the organisation. The current economic environment in Greece, combined with the pressures facing the Greek public sector, means that making this case is more important than ever.

> **IIA Standard 2030: Resource management**
>
> The chief audit executive must ensure that internal audit resources are appropriate, sufficient, and effectively deployed to achieve the approved plan.

Internal audits provide a vital review of the finances and operations of public sector institutions. Internal audit provides important services, such as detecting and preventing fraud, testing internal control, and monitoring compliance with government policy and regulation.

Making the business case for internal audit

Modernisation of the internal control framework within the Greek central public administration involves adopting a decentralised model, which necessitates a strong internal audit function.

Law 3492/2006 encourages ministries with budgets greater than EUR 3 million to have an internal audit function that follows IIA standards.

IIA standards require a sufficient number of auditors to address identified risk areas.

Governments lose millions of dollars every year to fraud. Law 3492/2006, Article 12 para. 2 of l. states: "A similar decision may establish internal audit units in the entities which supervised by the ministries or the decentralised administration of the country within the described in Article 3 the scope of this law and have a budget of over of three million (3 000 000) EUR [...]."

A formal internal audit unit that examines policies and procedures on a regular basis ensures that government minimises its exposure to fraud and other losses. Operational audits examine the efficiency of operations, which can be another area of significant losses for government. Is the organisation operating at maximum efficiency? Ineffective operations add to overheads without increasing results for Greek citizens. An operational audit may reveal these inefficiencies or point to unnecessary paperwork. Is the organisation following applicable regulations? Finding out that there is a lack of compliance with a government regulation ensures that elected officials maintain control and oversight. Government needs to monitor compliance with human resource laws to avoid costly mistakes. Internal audit performs a vital service in reviewing these functions.

Benchmarking information to support the size of an internal audit function can help to develop a business case for a strong, well-resourced internal audit function. There are a number of benchmarking studies available for comparison purposes; the most comprehensive is the IIA's GAIN survey, which identifies typical sizes of internal audit functions, the number of resources per organisation, and output expectations.[2]

2.2.2. Organisational design

Depending upon resource needs, a typical organisational structure involves two types of activities in an audit function: professional practices and audit operations. Professional practices typically involve resources devoted to quality assessment, strategic planning and reporting, and liaison with external auditors and other related external bodies, such as inspection bodies and the central agency responsible for co-ordinating internal audit:). Audit operations concern the planning, conduct and reporting of audit engagements. Depending upon the size of the organisation, audit operations typically have three levels of positions, in addition to the chief audit executive: the audit manager who leads audit engagements; auditors who undertake the actual audits; and entry level position(s) to assist in the conduct of audits.

Figure 2.4. Typical IA unit structure

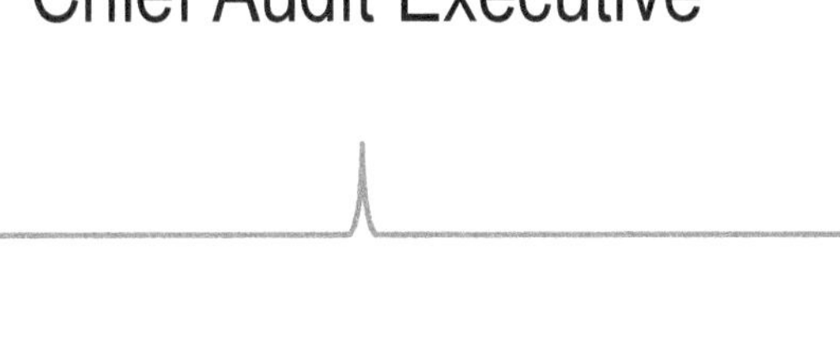

Source: Government of Canada (2014), Internal Audit Reference Centre, Internal Audit Sector, Office of the Comptroller General, Treasury Board Secretariat.

2.2.3. Competency profile

Figure 2.5 presents a competency profile targeted at the needs of the Greek public service. Articulating the necessary competencies of audit staff helps to develop job descriptions and design organisations. Most important, a competency-based management system supports the conversation that employees have with their supervisors about their present work and career aspirations by identifying elements that should be included in their learning plan.

Figure 2.5. IA Competency Framework

Knowledge Areas	Competencies	Entry Level	Auditor	Audit Manager	Chief Audit Executive
Technical skills	• IPPF understanding • Governance, risk and control specialist • Critical thinking • Research methodologies • Possesses area of specialisation (accounting, economics, statistics, etc...)	64%	39%	24%	13%
Business skills	• Strategy • Organisation building • Budgeting • Project management • Performance management	16%	24%	25%	25%
People skills	• Influence • Negotiation • Decision-making • Communication • HR skills (recruitment, staffing, and retention)	14%	21%	25%	23%
Leadership skills	• Team building • Coaching and mentoring • Driving performance • Motivating and inspiring • Change management	6%	16%	26%	39%

Source: Adapted from IIA (2015), Creating an Internal Audit Competency Process for the Public Sector, Institute of Internal Auditors.

Internal audit activity requires personnel from diverse backgrounds and different levels of experience. Smaller ministries will need to rely on more experienced auditors, while larger ministries will benefit from a blend of newcomers, seniors, and people from different academic and professional backgrounds.

IIA Standard 1210: Proficiency

"Internal auditors must possess the knowledge, skills, and other competencies needed to perform their individual responsibilities. The internal audit activity collectively must possess or obtain the knowledge, skills, and other competencies needed to perform its responsibilities."

Required audit competencies include:

- Proficiency in applying internal audit standards, procedures, and techniques. Proficiency means the ability to apply knowledge to situations likely to be encountered and to handle them without extensive technical research or assistance.
- Proficiency in accounting principles and techniques. Auditors who will work extensively with financial records and reports should be proficient in those areas.

- An understanding of management principles that enables auditors to recognise and evaluate the materiality and significance of deviations from sound business practices. An understanding means the ability to apply broad knowledge to situations likely to be encountered, to recognise significant deviations, and to carry out the research necessary to arrive at reasonable solutions.
- An appreciation of the fundamentals of subjects such as accounting, economics, commercial law, taxation, finance, quantitative methods, and IT. An appreciation means the ability to recognise the existence of problems or potential problems and to determine when further research should be undertaken or when to obtain expert assistance.
- Internal auditors should be skilled in dealing with people and in communicating effectively both orally and in writing.
- Another much appreciated skill is computing proficiency.

2.2.4. Accreditation and certification

Accreditation can be an important indicator of an auditor's technical proficiency. Certifications that have been recognised as showing technical proficiency useful in internal audit include: Certified Internal Auditor® (CIA®), Certified Public Accountant (CPA), and the Certified Government Auditing Professional® (CGAP®). An emphasis should be placed upon selecting persons with a CPA or the international equivalent (e.g. chartered accountant). The government should support their employees in obtaining IIA membership and achieving their CIAs. This can be done through financial support to pay for the test upon graduation, and/or providing up to 10 days on the job to study for the exams. The organisation benefits greatly from supporting the achievement of employee accreditation as they obtain the resources of a trained auditor, which is a rare commodity.

2.2.5. Job descriptions

Another important step in the hiring and/or appointment process is to develop detailed job descriptions for each position in the internal audit department; identifying the skills, knowledge, and abilities required. This ensures clear roles and responsibilities within the IA unit, and aids in the professionalisation of the audit function. Audit Tool #2 presents three basic types of job description: chief audit executive, audit manager/auditor, and an entry level auditor position. These job descriptions are based upon the competency framework presented in Figure 2.4. CAE positions are expected to have a full understanding of audit, as well as appropriate accreditation, such as an accounting degree, a CIA, a CGAP or similar qualifications.

2.2.6. Learning and professional development

The IIA Global Curriculum identifies nine core training areas, identified in Box 2.2. Chief audit executives need to support their employee's ongoing professional development. Once an auditor has a CIA, they are required to achieve a certain number of training hours per year. As the professional association for auditors, the IIA provides cheaper training opportunities for its members.

IIA Standard 1230: Continuing professional development

Internal auditors must enhance their knowledge, skills, and other competencies through continuing professional development.

Box 2.2. Recommended professional development training

1. Principles of internal auditing
2. Ethics and organisational governance
3. Fraud and forensics
4. Information technology (IT) auditing
5. Business communication skills for internal auditors
6. Internship and/or case studies/internal audit projects
7. Advanced internal auditing
8. Developing and managing an internal audit function
9. Risk management

Source: IIA Global Model Internal Audit Curriculum.

2.2.7. People performance measurement

The final component of the Audit People Management Framework is employee performance measurement. Being able to manage employee output is critical. Such performance measurement begins with chief audit executives who should report directly to the general secretary of the organisation.[3] At the beginning of the year, there should be a discussion on the CAE's objectives for the year and key deliverables on how performance will be measured. Midway through the year there should be a discussion between the General Secretary and the CAE in terms of how performance is going and if there is any need for adjustments. At the end of the year there should be a formal, written summary of the achievements made. This document would be signed by both the secretary general and the head of audit. It should identify achievements made over the year, areas requiring improvement, and future learning plans to support the CAE in delivering organisational objectives. This approach should then be replicated with each employee within the internal audit office.

2.3. Professional practices

IIA Standard 1300: Quality assurance and improvement programme

The chief audit executive must develop and maintain a quality assurance and improvement programme that covers all aspects of the internal audit activity.

Professional practices reflect the full set of policies, processes, and practices that enable the internal audit function to be performed effectively and with proficiency and due professional care. It refers to the capacity of the IA unit to align itself with the organisation's priorities and risk management strategies and contribute to the continuous improvement of IA activity and the organisation. It includes the development and maintenance of a quality assurance and improvement programme that covers all aspects of internal audit activity.

Each internal audit function must have a quality assurance and improvement programme (QAIP) so that the CAE can have confidence in the quality of audit reports and the recommendations being provided to senior management. Without a quality assurance programme, the CAE cannot have assurance that the findings of audit engagements are valid and reliable. Quality programmes include periodic internal and external quality assessments and ongoing internal monitoring. The IIA has a full QAIP manual that each CAE should be aware of and implement in their organisation. The programme is designed to help internal audit activity add value and improve the operations of the organisation, as well as to provide assurance that the activity conforms with the standards.

Quality programme assessments include the evaluation of:

- Conformance with the definition of internal auditing, the code of ethics, and the standards, including timely corrective actions to remedy any significant instances of non-conformance.
- Adequacy of the internal audit activity's charter, goals, objectives, policies, and procedures.
- Contribution to the organisation's governance, risk management, and control processes.
- Compliance with applicable laws, regulations, and other government standards.
- Effectiveness of continuous improvement activities and adoption of best practices.
- The extent to which internal audit activity adds value and improves the organisation's operations.[4]

Tailored codes of ethics are not needed. In fact, it is better to use the IIA Code of Ethics and have this reference made in an audit charter. This allows the CAE to refer to international standards and code of ethics, which provides increased independence and authority.

2.4. Governance structures

IIA Standard 1100: Independence and objectivity

The internal audit activity must be independent, and internal auditors must be objective in performing their work.

Interpretation: Independence is the freedom from conditions that threaten the ability of the internal audit activity to carry out internal audit responsibilities in an unbiased manner. To achieve the degree of independence necessary to effectively carry out the responsibilities of the internal audit activity, the chief audit executive has direct and unrestricted access to senior management and the board.

Objectivity is an unbiased mental attitude that allows internal auditors to perform engagements in such a manner that they believe in their work product and that no quality compromises are made. Objectivity requires that internal auditors do not subordinate their judgment on audit matters to others. Threats to objectivity must be managed at the individual auditor, engagement, functional, and organisational levels.

IIA Standard 1110: Organisational Independence

The chief audit executive must report to a level within the organisation that allows the internal audit activity to fulfil its responsibilities. The chief audit executive must confirm to the board, at least annually, the organisational independence of the internal audit activity.

IIA (2016), *International standards for the professional practice of internal auditing (standards)*, Institute of Internal Auditors.

Governance generally refers to the combination of processes and structures implemented by the board of directors and/or a supervising body (for example, an audit committee) to inform, direct, manage, and monitor the organisation's activities towards the achievement of its objectives.

Governance structure includes the administrative and functional reporting relationships of IA activity. It includes the CAE's reporting relationship to the governing body and how IA activity fits within the organisation's structure and governance regime. It also includes how the independence and objectivity of IA activity is assured, for example, through its formal mandate, legislated authority, and/or oversight mechanism, such as an audit committee.

Box 2.3. Who should internal audit report to?

Maintaining audit independence is vital for audit to add value to the organisation. Distinguishing between administrative reporting relationships versus functional reporting relationships can help support an independent audit function.

An administrative reporting relationship establishes a clear line of authority between positions or units in the organisational hierarchy. The actions of the subordinate are subject to the direction and/or approval of the next higher level of management, irrespective of the autonomy the latter may choose to grant to, or withhold from, subordinate levels.

A functional reporting relationship, on the other hand, establishes a connection between positions or organisational units at different management levels based on the specialised nature of the function for which a mutual responsibility is shared. In this situation – often referred to as an indirect reporting relationship – the higher level position or unit provides functional guidance and support to positions or units lower in the organisational structure.

Source: Cite HR (n.d.), Difference between administrative and functional reporting, www.citehr.com/404301-difference-between-administrative-functional-reporting.html.

The governance structure should provide an organisational framework so that the audit unit improves its chances of contributing effectively to the achievement of the organisation's mission, goals, and objectives.

Regardless of legislative frameworks, it is important that the purpose, authority, and responsibility of the internal audit function are formally defined in a charter. This supports understanding and buy-in by senior management, and can be used by the CAE to promoted increased access to information within the organisation.

Given the comprehensiveness and complexity of internal audit activities, the IA unit should have the requisite status within the organisation — otherwise other units within the ministry may not co-operate with the internal audit function. It is a primary concern to provide adequate, necessary status to the internal audit function. Therefore, the internal audit function should report directly to the highest management officials of the organisation, such as the General Secretary.

Internal audit activity should encompass every part of the organisation's operations, and to this end it should have unlimited access to the organisation's personnel, documents, records, and properties.[5]

Introducing audit committees into the Greek public service will help promote audit independence. These committees should be chaired by the most senior public servant in the organisation (i.e. general secretary), and consist of two to three key senior managers, plus one or two independent persons from an external body, such as the Court of Auditors and/or an inspection body.

Along with the appropriate level of organisational status, the internal audit department should have organisational independence. This means that the internal audit function should not have any direct relationships with the departments and/or functions that it will be auditing.

The internal audit charter provides the internal audit function with a formal mandate for its work. It should define the following items regarding the internal audit function:

- Establish the position of the internal audit department within the organisation and define the scope and nature of its activities.
- Authorise the internal auditors' access to, among other things, all records, personnel and property needed to accomplish audit and consulting projects.
- Grant the CAE the authority to allocate resources, establish schedules, determine the scope of audit work, and set audit objectives, without undue interference from management.
- Clearly outline the department's reporting structure, giving the CAE full and unrestricted access to senior management.
- Clearly communicate that the purpose of internal audit activity, as identified by the respective laws, is to serve the organisation by evaluating the effectiveness of risk management, control, and governance processes consistent with the IIA's definition of internal auditing, standards, and code of ethics. This also includes co-ordinating internal audit activities with others, such as the Court of Auditors and other inspection bodies, to achieve the most effective and efficient results.

IIA Standard 1311: Internal assessments must include:

• Ongoing monitoring of the performance of the internal audit activity.

• Periodic self-assessments or assessments by other persons within the organisation with sufficient knowledge of internal audit practices.

Organisational relationships and culture refers to the IA relationship with other units in the organisation. It includes the CAE's relationships with senior management and as part of the management team, as well as the ability to advise and influence top-level management and develop effective and ongoing relationships. It also refers to the IA unit's relationships with other review institutions, including the Court of Auditors and other investigatory bodies, such as the General Inspector of Public Administration.

2.5. Organisational relationships and culture

CAEs need to build relationships throughout the ministry by:

- Maintaining relationships throughout the organisation.
- Sitting on management committee meetings.
- Undertaking active communications throughout ministry on the importance and the role of IA.
- Conducting workshops and training on control, risk and governance.
- Assisting the organisation to become audit ready.
- Internal audit does not cover internal controls but provides assurance as to whether they are working and how they can be improved.

The CAE's role is to build relationships throughout the organisation. This requires active communications, including communication products, so that all employees have sufficient information to understand and appreciate the role of internal audit and know how it can benefit their respective units within the ministry. This requires individual briefings, as well as ministry-wide workshops and communication. Staff throughout the organisation should be actively engaged so that they understand the role and importance of internal audit.

Maintaining and building relationships is part of the advisory and consulting role of internal audit. If programmes and services do not understand their role in terms of developing, implementing and monitoring internal controls and using them to achieve better management and results, then it will be difficult to introduce internal audit into the organisation. To this end, internal audit needs to work with managers to help them become audit ready.

2.6. Performance management and accountability

Performance management refers to the information needed to manage, conduct, and control the operations of the IA activity and account for its performance and results.

It is vital that the CAE can demonstrate the value-added by internal audit. This includes the capacity to report on the effectiveness of IA activity to relevant stakeholders and the public. Being able to report regularly on audits produced and outcomes achieved is the biggest way to obtain senior management buy-in.

Public reporting of IA effectiveness

- IA operating budget
- IA business plan
- Performance measures
- Cost information
- IA management reports
- Integration of qualitative and quantitative performance measures

The CAE should also be able to ensure that the information collected through audits is protected. This includes the procedures to manage and protect the integrity of data, and to produce and present the appropriate information and results when needed.

Notes

[1] Adapted from IIA (2009), *IPPF Supplemental Guidance: Internal Audit Capability Model (IA-CM)*, Institute of Internal Auditors and IIA (2012), *IIPF Supplemental Guidance: Implementing a New Internal Audit Function in the Public Sector*, Institute of Internal Auditors.

[2] Table 2.2 and Figure 2.2 (pages 29 and 31) from Australian National Audit Office (2000), *Benchmarking the Internal Audit Function*, Australian National Audit Office.

[3] Currently, Law 3(N. 3492/2006, Article 12) requires that the head of audit report directly to the minister. As part of the recommended legislative modernisation, this reporting relationship would be clarified as only a function reporting relationship (i.e. minister provides broad direction and is a recipient of the information provided by the internal audit unit), whereas under the proposed new modernised legislation, the head of internal audit position would be elevated in level to that of a chief audit executive reporting to the public service head of the organisation, such as secretary general:. The secretary general would provide administrative direction and be the principal recipient of the information produced by the internal audit unit, positioning internal audit as a management function providing assurance regarding the governance, risk management and control frameworks within the organisation.

[4] IIA (2013), *Quality Assessment Manual,* Institute of Internal Auditors.

[5] IIA (2012), *IIPF Supplemental Guidance: Implementing a New Internal Audit Function in the Public Sector*, Institute of Internal Auditors.

3. How to help programmes and services get audit ready

This section provides guidance and checklists to facilitate the self-assessment of internal control systems and management practices. Its purpose is to enable decision makers to demonstrate strong fiscal stewardship and identify areas requiring improvement prior to undertaking a formal internal audit. It enables programme managers to be accountable for the internal control systems under their responsibility and helps them become audit ready.

3.1. Internal control frameworks

Internal control is an integral process that is affected by an entity's management and personnel and is designed to address risks and provide reasonable assurance that the following general objectives are being achieved in pursuit of the entity's mission:

- Executing orderly, ethical, economical, efficient and effective operations.
- Fulfilling accountability obligations.
- Complying with applicable laws and regulations.
- Safeguarding resources against loss, misuse and damage.

Internal control and internal audit are not synonymous. Internal control, as stated above, is an ongoing management function, while internal audit is an episodic formal review of how well management and staff are carrying out their responsibilities. Internal audit units are often asked to examine how well internal control within an organisation is being conducted.

Internal control is synonymous with the term "management control", with primary responsibility resting with the management of the executing ministry and its subordinate organisations, although it requires participation by all employees. It is a major part of managing an organisation and should be sufficiently flexible to allow the ministry and organisations to tailor control activities to fit their special needs. An assessment of internal controls therefore requires a review of specific mechanisms or systems for managing risks and the overall administrative and management environment.

3.2. How to undertake a control self-assessment

Internal control is not a separate system, instead it should be an integral part of each system or process that management uses to regulate and guide its operations. Internal control is management control built into the entity's infrastructure to help managers run the entity and achieve their aims on an ongoing basis.

Because internal control is one of the most important functions of management, it is important that managers have a basis for regularly assessing whether the organisation's internal control processes are achieving their objectives. Management should not be limited to formal assessments conducted by others. Audits of an organisation's internal control processes are generally conducted annually or less frequently. It would be helpful for management to have regular assurance that its internal control processes are functioning at an adequate level on an ongoing basis. This would allow management to identify potential problems before they escalate to major issue status, rather than waiting until they are identified by internal and external audits. Because self-assessments are less detailed and thus less time consuming and resource intensive, they can be conducted more frequently. Since internal control is the responsibility of everyone in the organisation, conducting self-assessments allows more people to feel ownership of the process. Such a process allows management to:

- Participate in the identification and assessment of risks.
- Develop remediation action plans.
- Assess the likelihood of achieving the organisation's objectives.
- Measure, monitor, and report on financial input and outcomes.

The output of the self-assessment tool is a snapshot of the relative strengths and weaknesses of the control environment. The assessment does not diagnose the reasons for weak or insufficient controls, but can pinpoint areas for further investigation. In addition to the completed worksheet, a written assessment report can be helpful in providing a summary of the entire process and main findings. Such a report would include the following sections:

- **Background** - Detailing the context in which the assessment is taking place, major changes or initiatives to address internal controls, the scope and scale of the assessment, and the description of the units being reviewed.
- **Objectives** - Stating the rationale for the self-assessment and the intended use of the findings.
- **Methodology** - Describing the specific scope of the assessment team, the justification for selection of the specific indicators, and the sampling methodology for data collection.
- **Strengths** - Summarising the areas where internal controls are sufficient, and how that assessment was made.
- **Weaknesses** - Detailing the areas where internal controls are insufficient or weak, and how that assessment was made.
- **Change over time** - If the assessment is being completed regularly, identifying any significant changes, either positive or negative.
- **Next steps** - Describing how the results of the self-assessment will be used to inform efforts to strengthen internal controls.

Box 3.1. Implementing a ministry-wide control self-assessment process[1]

Employing a self-assessment methodology can help instil a level of ownership of both the review process and the findings. It can also aid with internal communication. Communication to internal stakeholders ideally takes place at three stages of the self-assessment process:

1. **Design:** An initial meeting or workshop with officials from throughout the organisation to launch the assessment is important in establishing transparent communication about the assessment process and potential results. The meeting/workshop should be designed to encourage feedback from participants on the assessment design, which would further increase buy-in from internal stakeholders. During this meeting, participants can be provided with talking points to share with their colleagues.
2. **Implementation:** During the self-assessment the team should be prepared to engage with colleagues about internal controls. The review is an opportunity to engage a broad set of stakeholders on the importance of internal controls, factors that make a good internal control and the findings from the data collection effort. This is particularly important in assessing the difference between practice and policy.
3. **Results:** The results of the assessment need to be communicated clearly and transparently. Senior leadership should focus on prioritising the actionable steps to be taken to strengthen internal control weaknesses, and highlighting those areas where management systems or procedures are not working. Sharing broadly with other staff is important to build accountability for improving internal controls and management systems.

The completed control self-assessment worksheet should be submitted to the head of internal audit for review. Internal audit will provide a challenge function, review the ratings and ask for supporting evidence where necessary. Most important, the internal audit unit will then summarise the findings of all worksheets across the ministry and create an audit readiness report.

Note

[1] USAID (2013), *Self-assessment of internal control health sector a toolkit for health sector managers*, this publication was produced for review by the United States Agency for International Development. It was prepared by Bruce Long and Jeremy Kanthor for the Health Finance and Governance Project.

4. How to build a risk-based audit plan (RBAP)

This section presents how to systematically assess risk and focus the priorities of IA activity's periodic audit and services plan on risk exposures throughout the organisation. The audit plan is one of the most critical tools developed by an internal audit unit. The value-added by internal audit starts with understanding the strategy and objectives of the ministry and then determining how their achievement can be best supported by internal audit. The first question is: "What are your ministry's objectives and how can internal audit support these priorities?"

As outlined in Figure 4.1 below, there are six steps to developing an audit plan. This section examines each of these steps. First, is to identify the audit universe, i.e., all the possible entities and activities to be audited within the organisation. Second, is to identify all possible risks associated with the audit universe. Third, is prioritising these risks based upon their importance, as not all risks can be addressed due to resource constraints. Fourth, is linking critical risks with the associated audit entity or activity to be addressed, and prioritising the audit projects or engagements that will be undertaken. Fifth, is to implement the audit plan. Sixth, is reporting on the success and challenges associated with implementing the audit plan.

> Developing a risk-based audit plan does not need to be complicated. Depending upon the level of IA maturity, for some organisations it consists of a workshop discussion on risk and audit priorities which are then submitted for consideration to some form of governance body, such as senior management or audit committee. The approach presented here provides a more rigorous approach to enhance audit plan validity and reliability to ensure scarce audit resources are effectively used.

These six steps should be undertaken while keeping in mind existing organisational risk analysis and government and senior management objectives, strategy, and expectations, as well as potential internal and external risk threats. Risk analysis does not need to be complex, and can involve information collection activities, such as surveys, interviews or workshops.

The most important factor to consider when developing the audit plan is the value-added from internal audit. As the saying goes, "if you do not make it simple for leaders to value internal audit, they probably won't." To do this, it needs to be ensured that the audit plan supports the organisation's strategic goals and objectives. Obtaining senior management engagement and approval of the plan can help achieve this goal. Key outputs and outcomes this section seeks to promote include:

- A periodic internal audit and services plan based on risk exposures throughout the organisation.
- Communication of risk and control information to appropriate parties within the organisation.

- Understanding the organisation's risks and opportunities and contributing to their mitigation by management, thereby improving overall risk management and control systems.
- Documented procedures for conducting the periodic risk assessment.
- Training information on risk-based audit planning.

Figure 4.1. Overview of a risk-based audit plan

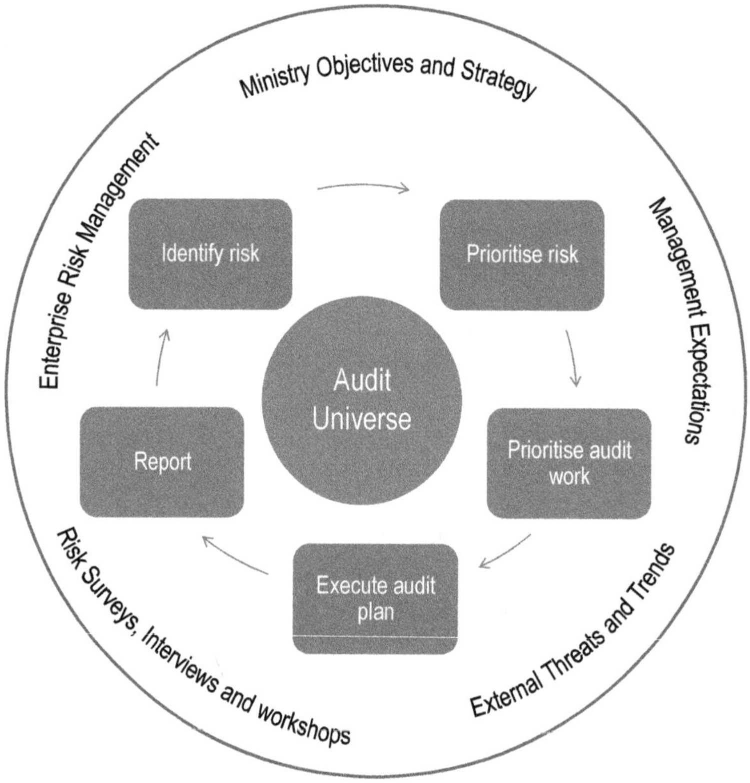

Source: Adapted from: Richard Arthurs, CMA, MBA, CIA, Former Chair of IIA Canada https://chapters.theiia.org/calgary/Documents/An%20Innovative%20Internal%20Audit%20Plan.pdf.

IIA Standard 2010: Planning

The chief audit executive must establish a risk-based plan to determine the priorities of internal audit activity, consistent with the organisation's goals.

Interpretation:

To develop the risk-based plan, the chief audit executive consults with senior management and the board and obtains an understanding of the organisation's strategies, key business objectives, associated risks, and risk management processes. The chief audit executive must review and adjust the plan, as necessary, in response to changes in the organisation's business, risks, operations, programmes, systems, and controls.

IIA (2016), *International standards for the professional practice of internal auditing (standards)*, Institute of Internal Auditors.

4.1. Identifying risk

The internal audit plan is intended to ensure that internal audit coverage adequately examines areas with the greatest exposure to the key risks that could affect the organisation's ability to achieve its objectives. As noted above, the IIA standard directs the chief audit executive (CAE) to start preparing the internal audit plan by consulting with senior management and any existing audit committee to understand the organisation's strategies, business objectives, risks, and risk management processes. This ensures that the CAE considers the maturity of the organisation's risk management processes.

4.1.1. Audit universe

The first step in any audit planning process is the identification of the audit universe. Although there are some commonalities between organisational audit universes, each organisation's will fundamentally be unique. Commonalities include certain typical management activities, as shown in Box 4.1.

Box 4.1. Overview of an audit universe

1. Management framework
2. Planning and accountability
3. Asset and resource management
4. Human capital management
5. Safeguarding of assets, information and people
6. Management of information and information technology
7. Legal services
8. Communications
9. Delivery of programmes and services

Audit tool #7 provides an example audit universe as a starting point. The audit universe includes projects and initiatives related to the organisation's strategic plan, and may be organised by business units, product or service lines, processes, programmes, systems, or controls. It is important to start with organisational strategies and goals as the foundation to avoid the risk of proposing irrelevant projects and not providing insight that management will truly care about. Most CAEs find that asking the internal audit standard question "what could go wrong?" to someone responsible for the strategic goals and objectives of the organisation immediately identifies new audit projects that may not have been considered.

Some organisations may use a formal risk management framework to assess, document, and manage risk; however, these are often created by auditors where they do not already exist. Once up and operating from one year to the next, this function is often taken over by management corporate services. Figure 4.2 below presents the process of identifying, assessing and prioritising risks.

Figure 4.2. Prioritising risk

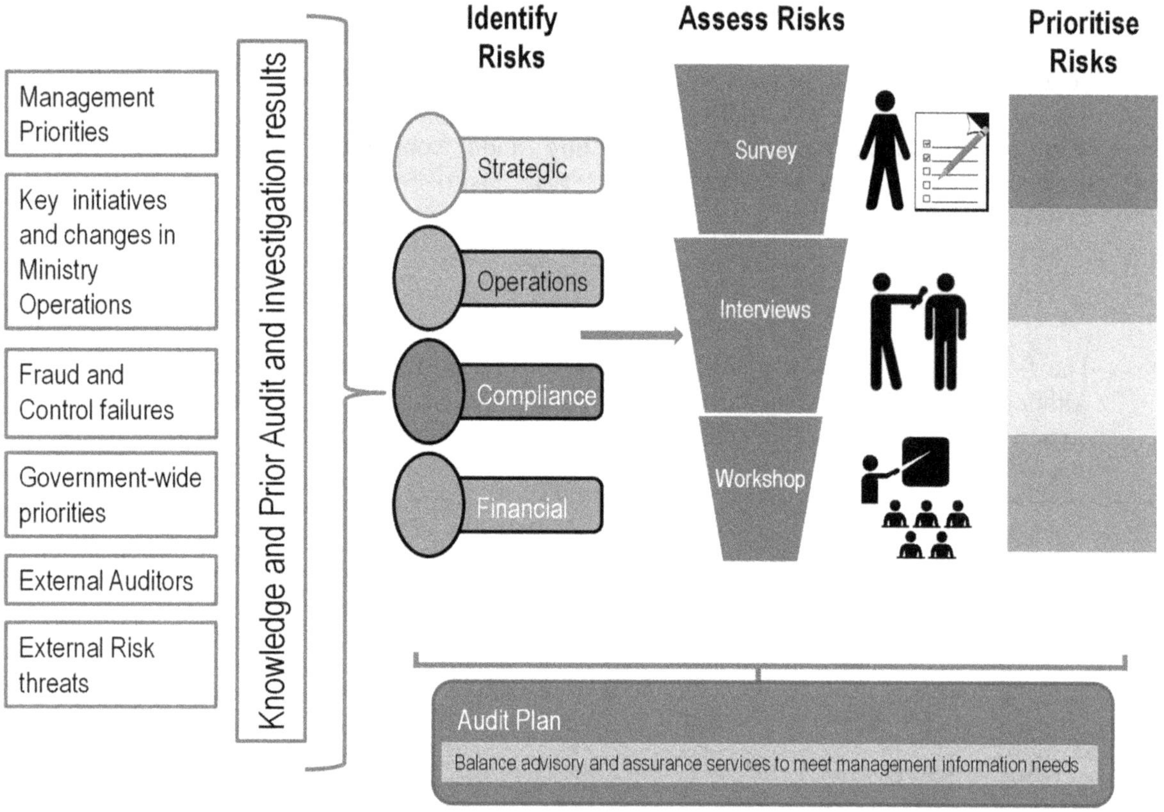

Source: Adapted from Ernst & Young.

The CAE can start by examining existing resources that identify risk. These include understanding management priorities based upon official organisational objectives, mission statements, and reports. CAEs need to be aware of any key initiatives or changes in ministry operations. They should also be aware of any past fraud or control failures that have occurred. Understanding government-wide priorities and how the ministry's objectives support them is critical. A full scanning should also be done of any external audit work, including a thorough review of any previous internal audit or investigation work undertaken. External risk threats, such as economic conditions, international relations, and European Commission priorities, should also be taken into account.

When conducting the risk assessment, the CAE should examine ministry activities from the perspective of measuring different types of risks, such as those identified in Figure 4.3 below. Strategic risks are those that could limit the achievement of ministry objectives or special initiatives. Operational risks are incidences that could impair the delivery of the ministry's core activities, services, programmes or deliverables. Financial risks involve the ability to deliver ministry activities within budget, potential resource constraints or financial reporting issues. Finally, there are risks pertaining to compliance with existing legislative, regulatory, or policy frameworks.

Primary audit activities should be on control and compliance issues,[1] i.e. providing assurance as to the efficiency and effectiveness of management controls and their compliance. Where resources permit, a second value-added focus should be auditing the management performance issues of efficiency and effectiveness. A third area for consideration is auditing emerging risks to help the organisation anticipate change and promote innovation, as well as achieve their strategic objectives, such as citizen focused services.

To determine whether there are risks in each of these areas, as well as their potential impacts, CAEs may employ a variety of information gathering tools, such as interviews, surveys, meetings, and workshops to gather additional input about the risks from management at various levels throughout the organisation, as well as from the board and other stakeholders. In most situations in Greek ministries, there will be limited or no access to quantitative risk information, but through qualitative methods, a risk profile can be developed and maintained over time. This will be further discussed later in this section.

Contrary to popular belief, senior executives should not be the first individuals sought for interview when performing a risk assessment. Instead, it is best to consider starting with a senior manager or director level employees.

Meetings with mid-level managers should involve asking how their roles and responsibilities help the organisation achieve its goals and objectives, and obtaining an understanding of how they spend most of their time. Questions should also be asked about whether they have increased headcount or resources, and if so, why, for example attrition, starting new projects or a new need for specialised knowledge. These reasons may quickly identify a key initiative of senior management that could benefit from independent insight and assurance.

It is important to take care during these interviews as some interviewees may attempt to identify projects or responsibilities that are important to the organisation, but are not their responsibility. The CAE should realise that the business manager may be attempting to avoid internal audit and keep the focus on the interviewee's responsibilities, not colleagues in other departments.

4.2. Prioritising risk

Audit Tool #6 is a sample risk collection and assessment tool. Initial factors or criteria that should be considered when measuring risk include: the complexity of the entity; the materiality of the organisation, i.e., its size and amount of resources; frequency of change in the entity, as change can lead to instability, change in personnel and hence a loss of upstanding and corporate memory; legal considerations in terms of the sensitivity of the organisation's legal framework; and any potential reputational risks.

To ascertain the relative risk ranking, each risk needs to be examined relative to each other. Figure 4.3 presents an overview of this approach. It involves examining the potential impact of a risk in relation to the estimated potential of the risk occurring. Together, these risks can be mapped out to distinguish between high versus low risks.

Figure 4.3. Mapping risk

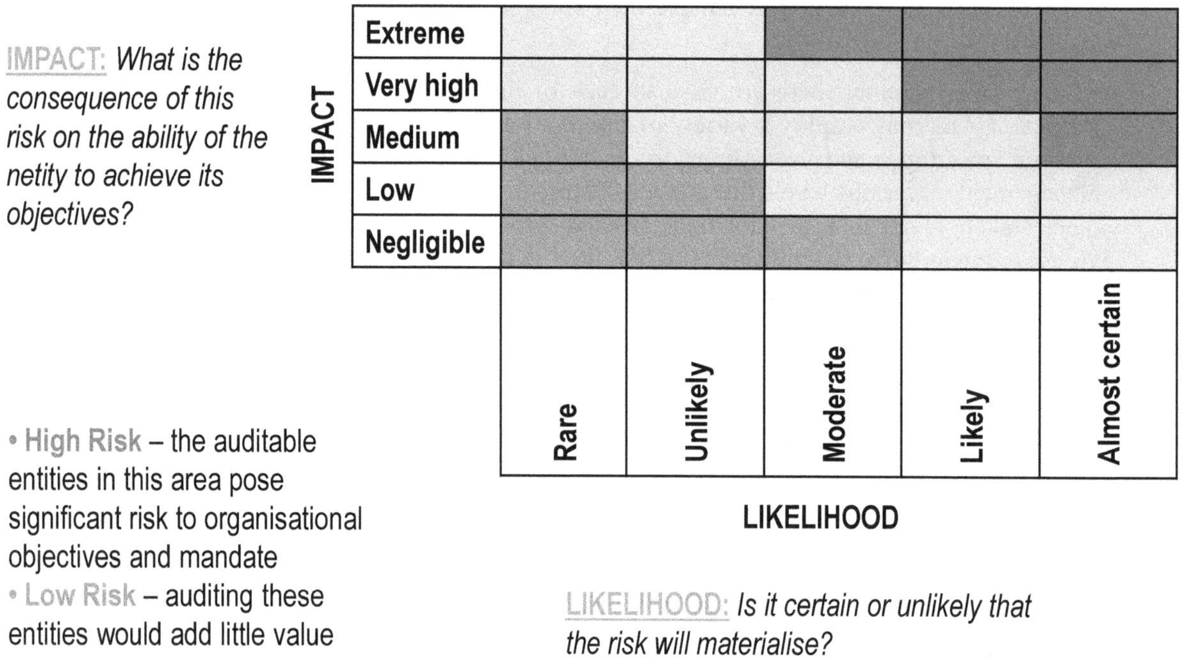

IMPACT: *What is the consequence of this risk on the ability of the netity to achieve its objectives?*

IMPACT					
Extreme					
Very high					
Medium					
Low					
Negligible					
	Rare	Unlikely	Moderate	Likely	Almost certain

LIKELIHOOD

- High Risk – the auditable entities in this area pose significant risk to organisational objectives and mandate
- Low Risk – auditing these entities would add little value

LIKELIHOOD: *Is it certain or unlikely that the risk will materialise?*

Source: Canada School of Public Service - Treasury Board Secretariat.

4.3. Prioritising audit work

The senior management team should be best placed to articulate the biggest risks in the organisation. It is best to provide them with plenty of information and feedback for their comment and consideration, as opposed to starting the risk assessment process with their interviews.

Once the key senior executives are in a room talking about what they deem to be the highest risk areas of the organisation, developing the future internal audit plan should be one of the easier tasks to complete. While there may be valid reasons for an executive to push back on a proposed project that aligns to their self-assessed key risks, most would find it difficult to permanently push back on the audit after they, along with their peers, deemed the risk as being key.

As illustrated in Figure 4.4 below, once risks have been identified and linked with the audit universe, these projects need to be prioritised by balancing risk issues with strategic value to the organisation. The projects then need to be further prioritised in terms of available resources, since it is rare to have enough resources to audit everything. Once these steps have been taken, the resulting list constitutes the audit plan. Once the proposed audit plan is finalised, it is important to summarise why each project is on plan. If each element is well justified, there should be little reason, if any, for the entire audit plan not being accepted.

Figure 4.4. Prioritising audit projects

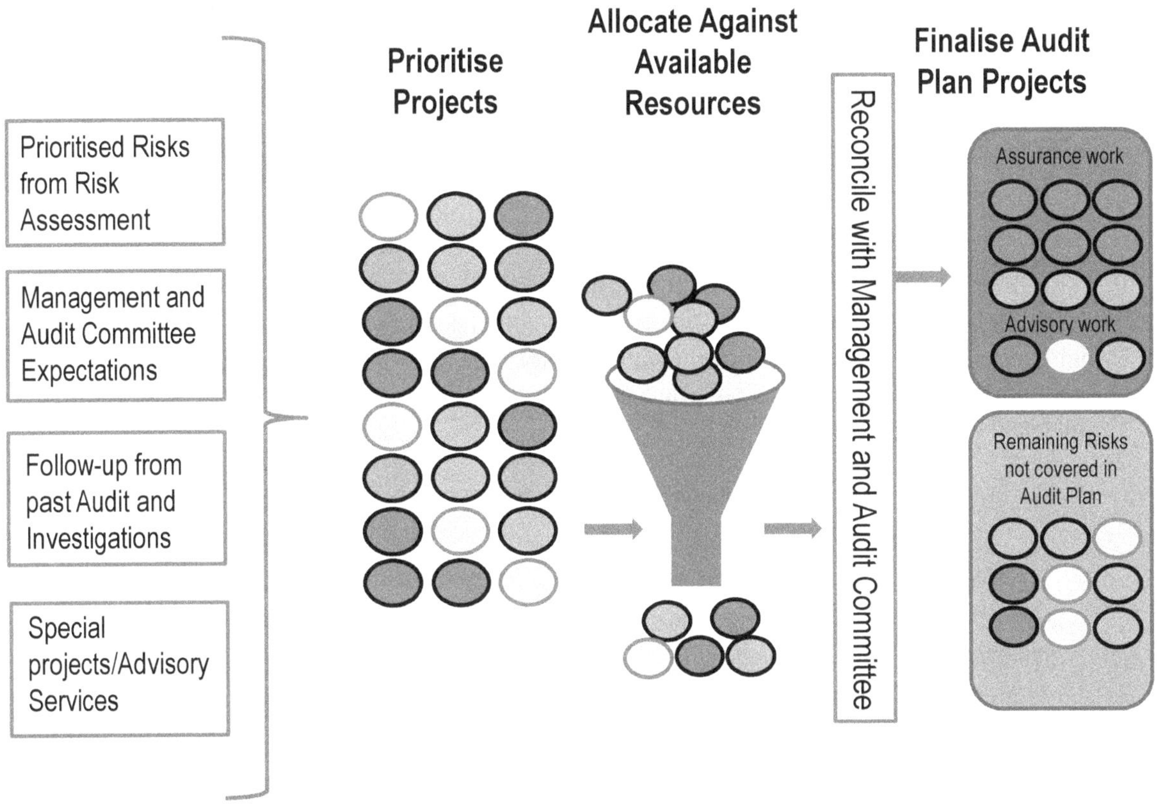

Source: Adapted from Ernst & Young.

4.3.1. Assurance mapping

When developing the internal audit plan, the CAE should consider any requests made by senior management, as well as the ability of internal audit activity to rely on the work of other internal and external assurance providers (as per Standard 2050). It can be useful to consider the first and second lines of defence in an organisation's control framework when determining which audit projects to initiate.

Figure 4.5 below provides an example of the key steps when undertaking an assurance map. Linking critical risks to specific objectives and business processes helps the CAE organise the audit universe and prioritise the risks. These risks are then analysed in terms of any existing controls that may exist to determine any gaps, i.e., the assurance activities of an organisation are mapped out to identify any gaps that audit may want to focus upon. The CAE uses a risk-factor approach to consider both internal and external risks. Internal risks may affect key products and services, personnel, and systems. Relevant risk factors related to internal risks include the degree of change in risk since the area was last audited, or the quality of controls. External risks may be related to political instability, fiscal environment or geopolitical issues. Relevant risk factors for external risks may include pending regulatory or legal changes and other political and economic factors.

To ensure that the audit universe covers all the organisation's key risks (as much as possible), internal audit activity typically independently reviews and corroborates the key risks identified by senior management.

Once information has been gathered and reviewed, the CAE develops an internal audit plan that usually includes:

- A list of proposed audit engagements (and specification regarding whether the engagements are assurance or consulting in nature).
- Rationale for selecting each proposed engagement (e.g., risk rating, time since last audit, change in management).
- Objectives and scope of each proposed engagement.
- A list of initiatives or projects that result from the internal audit strategy, but that may not be directly related to an audit engagement.

Although audit plans are typically prepared annually, they may be developed according to another cycle. For example, internal audit activity may maintain a rolling 12-month audit plan and re-evaluate projects on a quarterly basis. Or, it may develop a multi-year audit plan and assess the plan annually.

Figure 4.5. Assurance mapping

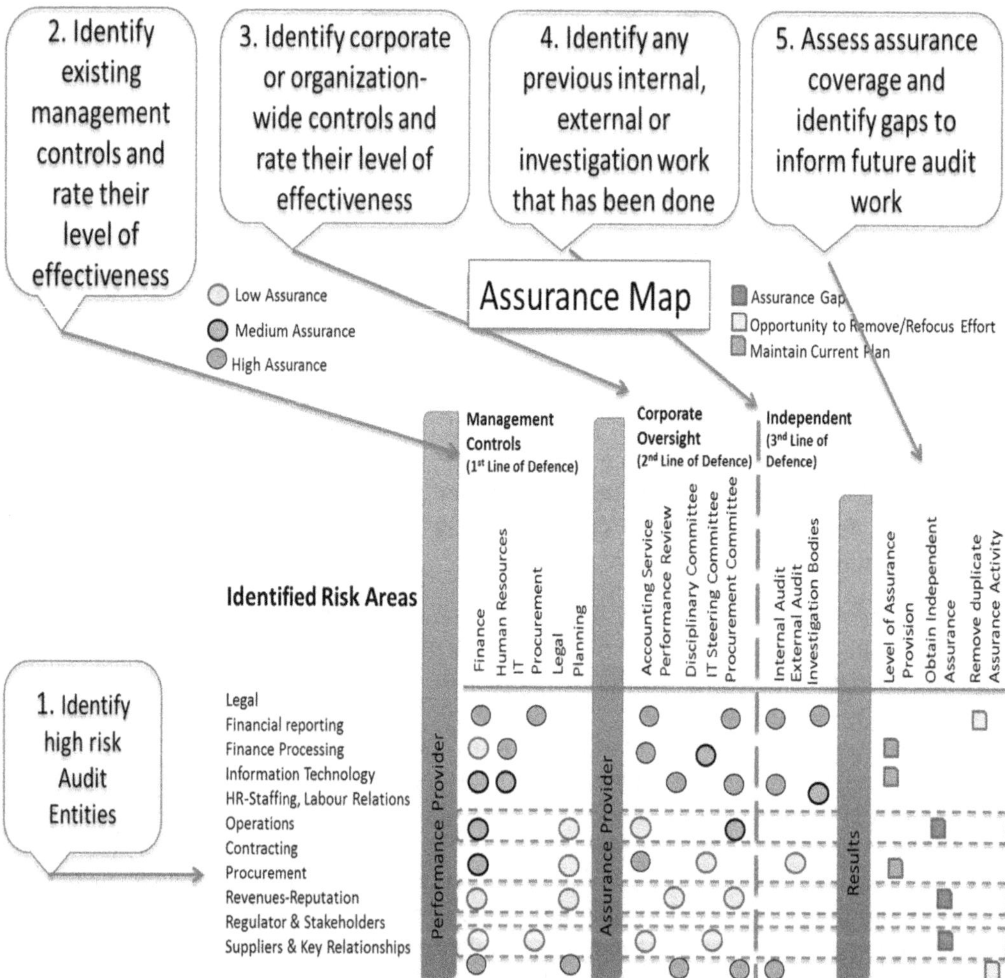

When the CAE discusses the internal audit plan with senior management, he or she should acknowledge risk areas not addressed in the plan. For example, this discussion may be an opportunity for the CAE to review the roles and responsibilities of senior management related to risk management, and the standards related to maintaining the independence and objectivity of internal audit activity (Standard 1100 to Standard 1130.C2). The CAE reflects on any feedback received from stakeholders before finalising the plan.

The internal audit plan should be flexible enough to allow the CAE to review and adjust as necessary in response to changes in the organisation's business, risks, operations, programmes, systems, and controls. Significant changes must be communicated to senior management for review and approval, in accordance with Standard 2020.

Figure 4.6. Living with risk

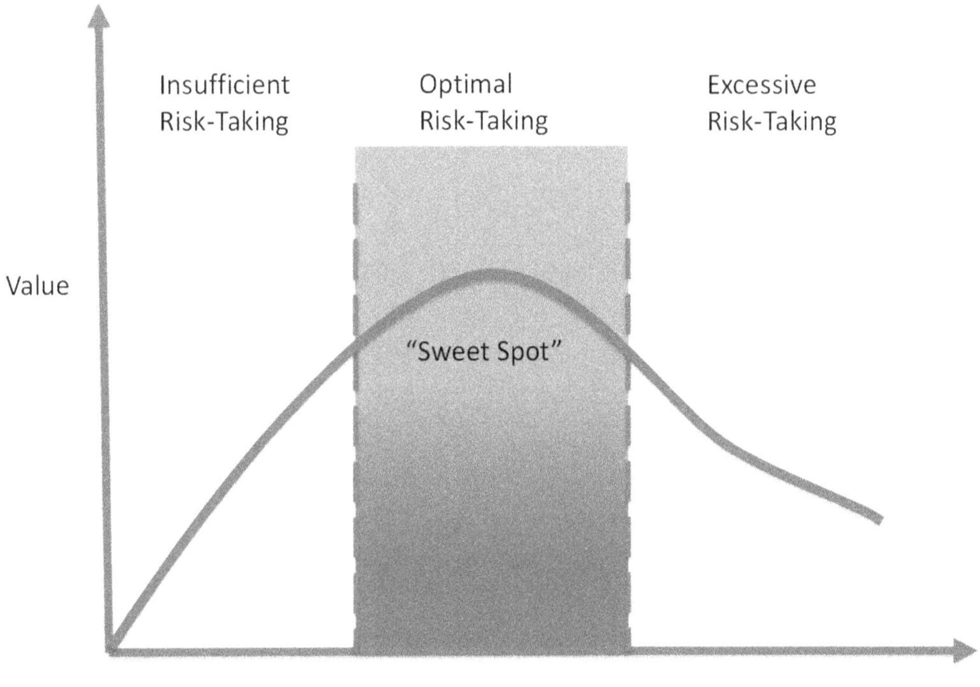

4.4. Reporting on the audit plan

Reporting on the accomplishments of the internal audit function is an opportunity to demonstrate the value-added by internal audit. The CAE should regularly report to senior management and the ministry audit committee on accomplishments. This should include outputs such as audit and consulting services provided, as well as impacts such as savings recovered from found billing errors, how the function supported strategic decision making, how audit supported enhanced cyber security, or how audit assisted in the identification of fraud.

Note

[1] IIA standards say that over 50% of activities need to be assurance focused and define what assurance is.

5. Internal audit and fraud

Sound management practices, strong public service values, and clear rules are key elements to combatting fraud. As values are fundamental to guiding sound management decisions, Greek citizens look both to the results achieved and to the means used when assessing government accountability.

This section focuses on the role and responsibilities of internal audit regarding fraud risk, and describes what auditors should do if there is a suspicion or allegation of fraud during an audit engagement. It highlights the important role of internal audit in fraud detection and the important relationship between internal audit and inspection-investigation bodies. It also highlights how internal audit can support the prevention and detection of fraud through considering fraud risk when developing the risk-based plan and when performing individual audits. This document also provides chief audit executives (CAEs), senior officials, and other key stakeholders with guidance on the role that internal audit plays in assessing ministry capabilities related to the prevention, detection, investigation, and reporting of possible acts of fraud. However, it does not presume or recommend that CAEs, in their internal audit role, are responsible for the detection or investigation of fraud, as this is the role and competence of inspection bodies.

IIA standard 2120.A2: Internal audit activity must evaluate the potential for the occurrence of fraud and how the organisation manages fraud risk.

Chief audit executives contribute to the fight against fraud in two ways:

1. Evaluate the ministry's fraud risk management and prevention activities, including fraud awareness programmes, employee training, communications, and policies and procedures on fraudulent activities. The CAE can contribute to a reduction in fraud risk by ensuring that adequate fraud risk management strategies are in place to discourage the commission of fraud and to minimise losses should it occur.
2. Ensure that fraud risk is thoroughly assessed during audit engagement planning.

5.1. Relationship between internal audit and forensic auditing

The purpose of an internal audit is to make recommendations for improving governance, risk management, and control processes. The purpose of a fraud investigation is to either confirm or refute the suspicion or allegation of fraud. Should the investigation conclude that fraud has occurred, its results will be used to support the prosecution of the person or persons committing the fraud. While internal auditors may uncover a potential fraud, their involvement stops at the point when a suspicion or allegation of fraud is deemed to be a probable fraud. At this point, the investigation would be performed by the fraud investigation team.

The skillset and tools required to perform a fraud investigation are not the same as those required for an internal audit. Therefore, internal audit is often not equipped to perform a fraud investigation, and CAEs must understand the difference between an internal audit and a fraud investigation.

The differences between internal audits and fraud investigations exist at many levels, starting with the timing of the activities and their initial assumptions. Table 5.1 outlines some of the major differences between internal audits and fraud investigations.

Table 5.1. Differences between internal audits and fraud investigations

Characteristic	Internal audit	Fraud investigation
Timing	• Based on risk	• Based on allegation or suspicion
Objective	• Opinion on governance, risk management, and controls	• Information for judicial and disciplinary proceedings

CAEs and senior management need to give careful consideration to the possibility of fraud occurring and to the assignment and communication of the roles and responsibilities for preventing, detecting, investigating, reporting on, and correcting possible acts of fraud.

CAEs need to understand the difference between inappropriate actions, wrongdoing, and fraud, as well as recognise that control weaknesses can lead to fraud. These actions can be caused by many factors, including lack of knowledge, gaps in oversight, difficulties in interpreting and applying policies and regulations, and deliberate actions. A detailed analysis of the situation may be required to identify the cause and effect of a wrongdoing and to decide on any required remedial or disciplinary measures to prevent it from developing into an act of fraud.

In the Institute of Internal Auditors' (IIA) International Standards for the Professional Practice of Internal Auditing (Standards), fraud is defined as follows:

Any illegal act characterised by deceit, concealment, or violation of trust. These acts are not dependent upon the threat of violence or physical force. Frauds are perpetrated by parties and organisations to obtain money, property, or services; to avoid payment or loss of services; or to secure personal or business advantage.

IIA (2016), International standards for the professional practice of internal auditing (standards), Institute of Internal Auditors.

Given that little tolerance exists within the Greek government for fraud or wrongdoing involving taxpayer contributions or government assets, the effectiveness of controls and governance for the prevention, detection, investigation, and reporting of wrongdoing and possible fraud represents a key responsibility for ministries'senior executives and management.

5.2. Guidance to IA on undertaking a fraud risk assessment

As part of a fraud risk assessment, the CAE should ensure that the ministry has clearly defined and communicated the roles and responsibilities for preventing, detecting, investigating, and reporting on possible acts of fraud, as well as identified the position responsible for taking corrective actions when fraud is uncovered.

In their leadership role, ministers and secretaries general have an obligation to actively monitor management practices and controls in the ministry and to effect timely and effective remedial actions when significant deficiencies are identified.

Internal audit is an integral component of an organisation's overall governance and control system for deterring, detecting, investigating, and reporting on possible fraud. However, the internal audit function is not the sole mechanism responsible for conducting the full range of these activities.

Internal audit develops and implements an annual risk-based internal audit plan of engagements that enables the CAE to provide an annual statement of assurance on the effectiveness and adequacy of risk management, control, and governance processes. While the work performed to develop the annual plan includes activities for identifying and assessing fraud risk, it does not include specific responsibilities for deterring, detecting, investigating, and reporting on possible acts of fraud. However, since internal audits conducted may uncover possible acts of fraud, misconceptions can arise about the role of internal audit and auditors in detecting fraud. Internal auditors do not necessarily possess either the skills or the abilities of an individual whose primary responsibilities are detecting and investigating fraud. Internal audit's role is to identify fraud risk and provide reasonable assurance on the adequacy of the system of internal controls, but internal audit procedures cannot guarantee that fraud will be detected.

The CAE should ensure that the ministry’s senior management and internal audit staff have a clear understanding of the roles and responsibilities of internal audit in the prevention and detection of wrongdoing and fraud. The CAE should also ensure that senior management is aware that an internal audit may not detect existing fraud. In the conduct of internal audits, there is no initial assumption that fraud has occurred. By contrast, a fraud investigation typically starts with the assumption that fraudulent activities have taken place, and the purpose of the investigation is to confirm or refute the allegations.

Nonetheless, the CAE should be aware of the potential for fraud, and accordingly review the ministry’s fraud awareness and prevention processes, conduct an overall fraud risk assessment, and understand the ministry’s specific fraud risk exposure. The CAE should also ensure that internal auditors have the skills and knowledge necessary to recognise the signs of fraud, and that all parties have a clear understanding of the procedures to follow when a possible fraud is detected during internal audit.

6. How to undertake an audit

This section consists of three distinct phases: engagement planning, conduct, and reporting. Each of these complex phases involves many steps and are explored in detailed below.

6.1. Engagement planning

Planning is the cornerstone of successful auditing. Proper planning allows audit teams to define audit objectives, scope, criteria, and methodology. Planning also enables the auditor to gain a better understanding of the subject area. This includes understanding environmental complexities, alignment within the ministry, legislative foundations, and potential risk in order to ensure that audit focuses on areas where it can be of most value.

Box 6.1. Key activities and outputs for engagement planning

Activities

1. Initiate the audit
2. Gain an understanding of the audit entity
3. Identify the key risks
4. Develop the audit programme
5. Meet with senior management
6. Develop and approve the terms of reference

Key outputs

The planning stage of the audit should result in three key documents: a risk assessment, an audit programme and terms of reference.

- Risk assessment: ensures that the audit focuses on areas of greatest value and risk. It is supported by an in-depth analysis of all the information gathered to identify areas of greatest inherent risk.
- Audit programme: outlines how work is to be performed during an audit to achieve the specified objectives.
- Terms of reference: summarises the scope, objectives, timelines, and other key planning decisions to senior management and the programme or service being audited.

At the end of the planning process, audit teams should be able to clearly articulate what will be audited, why it will be audited, and how it will be audited.

Box 6.2. International Professional Practice Framework (IPPF): Planning phase

The Institute of Internal Auditors' Standards for Professional Practice of Internal Auditing outlines the following requirements:

- Internal auditors must develop and document a plan for each engagement, including the engagement's objectives, scope, timing, and resource allocations (Standard 2200).
- Objectives must be established for each engagement (2210).
- The established scope must be sufficient to satisfy the objectives of the engagement (2220).
- Internal auditors must determine appropriate and sufficient resources to achieve engagement objectives based on an evaluation of the nature and complexity of each engagement, time constraints, and available resources (2230).
- Internal auditors must develop and document working programmes that achieve the engagement objectives (2240).

Figure 6.1. Key activities in the planning phase

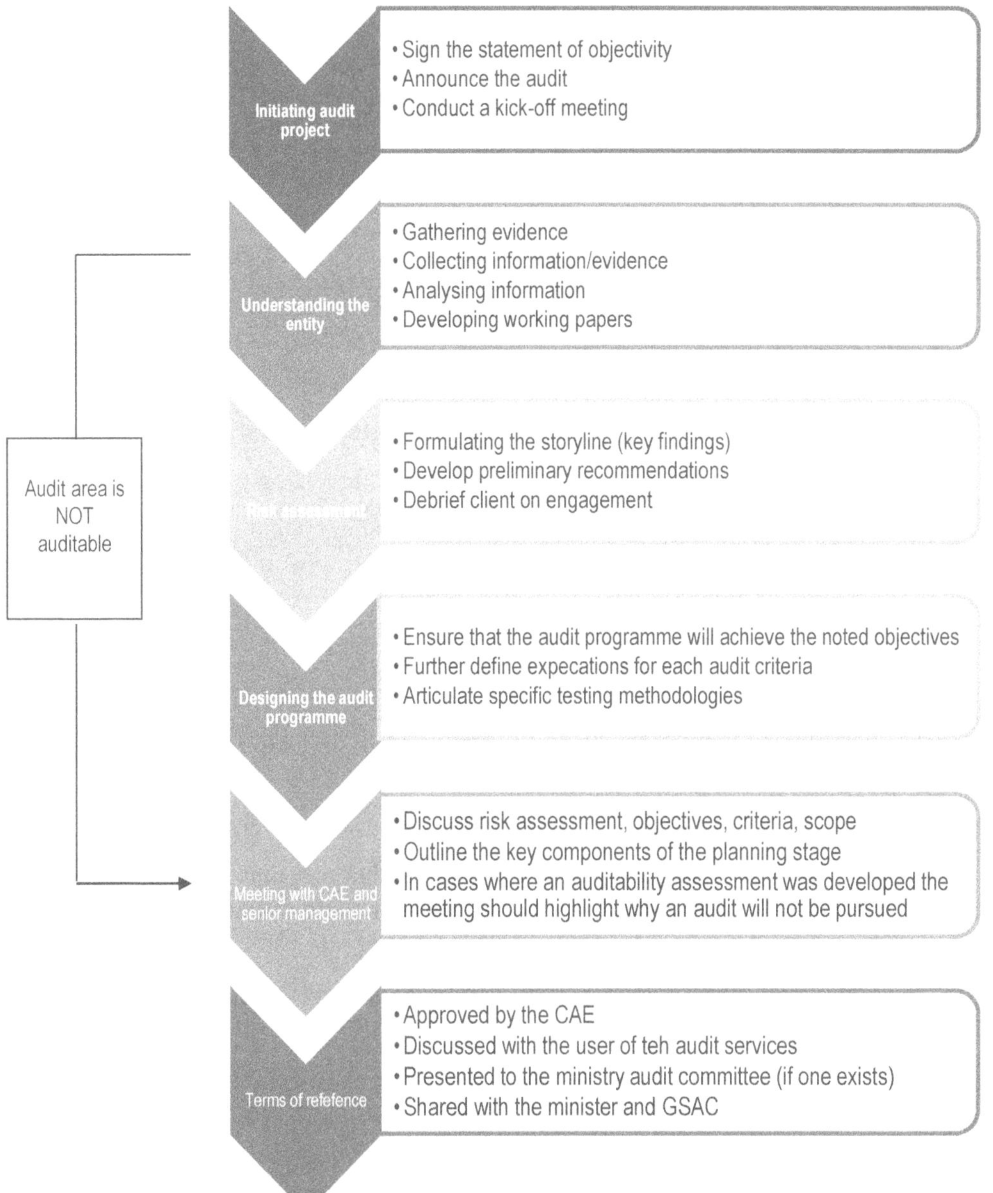

Source: Adapted from: Government of Canada (2016), Audit Manual, Human Resources and Development Canada, Government of Canada.

6.1.1. Initiating the audit project

The following activities should be completed during the initiation of an audit project to ensure that engagement is well planned and that the user of the services is informed in a timely manner.

Some techniques to consider when developing an audit approach:

- Process mapping and control analysis
- Data analysis
- Analytical review
- File review
- Surveys
- On-site observations
- System testing
- Documentation review (policies, operations manual, directives)
- Interviews

Statement of objectivity

Internal auditors must perform engagement in such a manner that they have an honest belief in their work product and that no significant compromises in quality were made. They must have an impartial and unbiased attitude and avoid any conflict of interest.

If the independence or objectivity of the auditor is impaired in fact or appearance, the details of the impairment must be disclosed to the audit principal or the level above, where applicable. The nature of the disclosure will depend upon the impairment. For example, the internal auditor's objectivity is impaired if the auditor is personally connected with the audit entity manager, or was involved in the design or implementation of the audit entity.

As per the Institute of Internal Audits' (IIA) code of ethics, internal auditors shall:

- Not participate in any activity or relationship that may impair or be presumed to impair their unbiased assessment. This participation includes those activities or relationships that may be in conflict with the interests of the organisation.
- Not accept anything that may impair or be presumed to impair their professional judgment.
- Disclose all material facts known to them that, if not disclosed, may distort the reporting of activities under review.

In order to mitigate the risk of non-objective assessments during an audit engagement, all auditors participating in a particular engagement must sign the statement of objectivity at the initiation of the planning phase. Any internal auditor that joins the team after the planning phase should also sign the statement of objectivity. All auditors need to sign the statement of objectivity and save it to the appropriate project file.

Announce the engagement

This is a simple and short step in the planning process that informs the client of the upcoming engagement and the reason for its inclusion in the risk-based internal audit plan. Announcing the engagement also opens the channel for the user of the services to contact internal audit senior management or the audit engagement principal to discuss the audit.

The audit team should draft an announcement memorandum that informs the user of the services that an assurance engagement is being initiated. The memorandum is sent from the CAE to the user of the services and indicates that the audit planning process has begun.

The memorandum must include the following:

- Launching of audit planning and seeking input from the user of the services.
- Announcing the name of the audit principal.
- Outlining the preliminary scope and objectives.
- Highlighting a kick-off meeting with the auditee.

The announcement memorandum template should be used to announce the audit. In order to complete this memo the following information is needed:

- Name(s) of the audit entity
- Title of engagement
- Date the annual risk-based audit plan was approved
- Engagement objective
- Approximate date the engagement will begin

Conduct a kick-off meeting

The audit team should meet the auditees to outline the audit process, preliminary audit objective, and scope. During this meeting, auditors should be prepared to discuss auditees concerns in relation to the engagement and the audit process, such as, the internal audit charter, and privacy considerations. This kick-off meeting should be formally documented.

Understanding the entity to be audited

To be able to complete and develop a comprehensive risk assessment that directs engagement to the areas of most value, the audit team needs to acquire a strong understanding of the entity being audited. The audit team's research and learning should focus on the objectives and the environment in which the audited entity operates. The information obtained will facilitate the assessment of the entity's inherent risks.

Sources of information

Information can sometimes be found on the ministry websites, which should be the first place researched by the audit team. The user of the services will have a more comprehensive set of information and documentation. It is important to have an open line of communication between the auditee and the audit team in order to facilitate the transfer and validation of information. When reviewing the information, auditors should begin noting potential risks that the audited entity may face.

A good starting point for this preliminary information is the entity risk profile worksheets. However, the audit team must venture deeper in understanding the business to identify key risks to a particular audit project.

Interviews and documentation reviews are the primary means of gathering this information. Interviews with the auditee can help identify objectives, roles, risks and the complexities of the environment in which the organisation operates.

Information management

All documentation and interview notes related to the engagement should be saved together. Being able to source all audit observations requires solid information management from the outset of the project. At the end of the audit, auditors should be ready to substantiate each audit finding if questioned.

Risk assessment

Internal audit teams need to understand the risks to management's key objectives and the controls to support targeted and value-added auditing. The information gathered and learnt at the "understanding the entity" stage supports the assessment of risk. Synthesising this information will equip the audit team with knowledge of the entity's business, its conditions, and what may predispose it to risk.

Determining the risks

Preliminary risk information within the entity profile sheet should provide audit teams with baseline risk information on the subject matter. However, it is important to note that the risk information is holistic in nature and not fully substantiated with an appropriate level of evidence, as required for audit engagements.

As part of audit's value added to senior management, a more comprehensive evaluation of risk needs to be conducted to ensure the proper identification of risk. The involvement of the user of the services can be beneficial, depending on the entity being audited.

The audit team should document the risks associated with the entity. The following information should be documented: key objectives, associated risks, likelihood of these risks, impact of the risks, and risk rating(s).

When identifying the risks associated with an engagement it is important to know the entity's business conditions that inherently predispose it to risk. Factors to be considered include:

- Degree of change.
- Degree of complexity and legislative requirements.
- Degree of dependencies and geographic dispersion.
- Degree of information technology dependencies and integration.

Documenting these elements ensures that the audit team has a clear rationale to conclude the engagement objective and scope.

In rare cases, the outcome of the risk assessment may highlight an issue or event that may lead the audit team to feel that engagement is not currently warranted. In this case, an auditability assessment, in addition to the risk assessment, must be prepared. The purpose of the auditability assessment is to provide the CAE, the auditee, and the MAC with the rationale for not moving forward with the engagement. The auditability assessment must reference the engagement objective and scope proposed in the annual risk-based audit plan, and include a detailed risk assessment section, and detailed next steps.

Designing the audit programme

Audit objectives are broad statements developed during the risk-based audit plan process that define the engagements' intended accomplishments. These objectives can be thought of as questions that auditors seek to answer. It is the responsibility of the audit principal, once the knowledge of business is completed, to re-evaluate the audit objectives to reflect the new information gathered. The resulting changes should be formally documented in a note to file.

In reconfirming objectives, the audit team should ask several questions to assess the feasibility of auditing certain areas:

- Do audit-subject activities lend themselves to audits?
- Do auditors have the required expertise, or can they acquire it?
- Will the audit add value to the organisation?
- Are audit subjects undergoing significant and fundamental changes?
- Are suitable criteria available to assess performance?

Scoping the engagement

The scope of an audit covers what will be audited. The scope statement should clearly describe the areas, processes, activities, or systems within the audited entity that will be the subject of the engagement and to which the audit conclusion will apply (including both the time period and the locations audited). It should also include the areas that will be out of scope.

The scope may be expressed in terms of the focus of the engagement (e.g. management framework, service delivery, operational processes, governance process, control systems). It will also note the branches and regions impacted and what period of time the audit will cover.

Any restrictions to the scope, and the reasons for these restrictions, should be described. Restrictions may occur, for example, when auditors are unable to audit key organisational units or systems, or are unable to perform necessary audit procedures as a result of factors beyond their control. The audit scope can also be limited by an inability to identify appropriate criteria.

Developing an audit programme

Once the risk assessment, scope, and objective(s) of the engagement have been finalised, the efficiency and quality of audits depend largely on how well audit programmes are designed and executed.

Example audit programmes: www.auditnet.org is a paid service with over 2000 audit programmes.

Audit programmes[1] are detailed plans outlining the steps to be performed during an engagement. The audit team should develop an audit programme that will achieve audit objectives and that aligns with the risks identified. The audit programme should contain audit objectives, criteria, and approach.

Audit criteria are reasonable and attainable standards of performance and control through which the entity can be evaluated and assessed. The criteria used will depend on the relevant risks observed by the audit team.

Criteria are generally found in the following areas: acts and regulations; government policy, guidelines or standards; risk management; management control framework information; standards developed by recognised professional organisations, acknowledged bodies of experts, and generally accepted operational standards or norms.

It is also considered best practice to indicate the sources of audit criteria in the audit programme. If there are no generally accepted criteria that relate to a given objective, but criteria from other sources have been identified, gaining the auditee's acceptance would be beneficial. If agreement on the criteria cannot be reached, the lack of agreement must be disclosed in the terms of reference, along with an explanation of why the audit team believes the criteria remains appropriate.

The following characteristics form good audit criteria:

- Understandable: clearly stated and not subject to significantly different interpretations by intended users.
- Relevance: contribute to findings and conclusions that meet audit objective(s).
- Reliability: result in consistent conclusions or opinions when used by different auditors in the same circumstances.
- Neutrality: free from bias that would cause auditors' findings and conclusions to mislead intended users of reports.
- Completeness: exist when all criteria that could affect practitioner's conclusions are identified or developed.

The audit approach refers to the work involved in gathering and analysing information to achieve audit objectives. This work ensures that sufficient and appropriate audit evidence is collected to enable audit teams to draw conclusions related to each audit criteria. The audit approach is intended to produce the most meaningful audit results for the users of the audit services in the most cost-effective manner. The audit team should use sound judgement when determining the audit approach.

When outlining the audit approach, audit teams should:

- Determine the evidence necessary to reach conclusions based on established criteria.
- Identify tests and other procedures needed to gather required evidence.
- Prioritise objectives so that high-risk processes are evaluated first.

It is important to consider all types of evidence available when developing a specific audit approach. Developing an audit approach that uses a combination of evidence from different sources and different types ensures that all possible conclusions are credible and supported by appropriate evidence.

Sampling plan

Sampling is a technique used to analyse data, or a portion of data, produced by the auditee. Sampling increases the efficiency and effectiveness of audits. Auditors should consider sampling techniques when developing specific audit steps.

There are two main types of sampling:

1. Statistical sampling: used to draw conclusions about populations. It permits auditors to project characteristics of the sample onto the population from which the sample is drawn. It also allows for the consideration of risk through the application of mathematical rules/formulas.
2. Judgmental sampling: used to establish the existence and determine the extent of suspected conditions. Non-statistical sampling is the selection of sample items without following structured techniques or established methods. Auditors cannot draw any conclusions about populations from directed samples beyond what is actually found.

When sampling is used as an audit step to evaluate the entity, it is important that the audit team document the methodology and get formal approval from the audit principal.

The audit teams need to define their sampling methodology in a plan that consists of:

- Sampling plan objective for the audit.
- Characteristics of the population.
- Selecting the sample methodology (i.e. statistical vs. judgemental approach, sampling size information, and sampling selection methodology).
- Documenting approach that will be used.
- Conclusion as to why this approach is appropriate.

Terms of reference

The terms of reference provides a high-level synopsis of the audit project to facilitate the auditee's understanding of the audit. It provides information on the scope, objective, approach and timing of the audit. This document is subject to challenge by the auditee.

Components of terms of reference

The terms of reference document ensures that auditees are aware of:

- audit objectives
- criteria and scope
- audit methodology
- sampling methodology
- internal audit responsibilities
- management responsibilities

- how audit findings will be communicated
- projected audit timelines.

Information management

The terms of reference should be shared with the auditee and presented to the MAC.

6.2. Conducting the Audit

The conduct phase officially commences upon the approval of the terms of reference. This phase of an audit involves collecting, examining, analysing and evaluating information pertaining to the engagement objective. This will allow the audit team to formulate conclusions on the state of the environment being audited. During this phase, the audit team executes the audit programme to:

- Obtain sufficient and appropriate evidence to support positive and negative conclusions for each audit objective.
- Determine the residual risk.
- Assess impacts and risks associated with non-conformity.
- Compare actual practice, operations or results with established frameworks.
- Identify opportunities to improve performance.

Box 6.3. Key activities and outputs in the conducting phase

Activities

1. Procedures were well communicated to the audit team.
2. Executing the audit programme: evidence is gathered in many forms to support audit analysis, findings, and conclusions.
3. Developing briefing material and briefing the client on the preliminary findings of the audit.

Key outputs

The conduct stage of the audit should result in the compilation of working papers and a meeting with the auditee to debrief them on the findings.

Box 6.4. International Professional Practice Framework (IPPF): Conduct phase

The IPPF outlines the following requirements for the conduct phase:

- Internal auditors must identify, analyse, evaluate, and document sufficient information to achieve the engagement's objectives (Standard 2300).
- Internal auditors must identify sufficient, reliable, relevant, and useful information to achieve the engagement objectives (Standard 2310).
- Internal auditors must base conclusions and engagement results on appropriate analyses and evaluations (Standard 2320).
- Internal auditors must document relevant information to support the conclusions and engagement results (Standard 2330).
- Engagement must be properly supervised to ensure objectives are achieved, quality is assured, and staff are developed (Standard 2340).

Source: IIA (2016), International Professional Practices Framework, Institute of Internal Auditors.

Figure 6.2. Summary of key activities for the conduct phase

Phase	Key activities
Initiating conduct phase	• Develop testing, tools, and guidance to ensure consistent application of audit programme. • Meet with the user of the services
Executing the audit programme	• Gathering evidence • Collecting information/evidence • Analysing information • Developing working papers
Engagement findings debrief	• Formulating the storyline (key findings) • Develop preliminary recommendations • Debrief quditee on engagement

Source: Adapted from: Government of Canada (2016), Audit Manual, Human Resources and Development Canada, Government of Canada.

6.2.1. Initiating the conduct phase

Tools and guidance should be developed to ensure that the audit teams consistently apply similar methodology to respond to audit criteria and approach. This helps the audit team achieve the intended engagement objectives.

Examples to support consistency include:

- file review checklists
- process review approach/plan
- sampling plan
- data test descriptions
- interview guide aimed at responding to questions extracted from the audit programme
- definitions of key words.

There are times during the execution of the audit programme when the approach needs to be changed. Changes can occur as the audit team gains greater knowledge of the processes and subject matter.

This new knowledge can support the continuous improvement of the audit approach and supporting tools to respond to the audit criteria. The audit team must document any changes to the audit approach or supporting tools.

Information management

Tools such as the interview guide, file review checklists and interview notes for the initial meeting with management should be saved under the correct project file.

6.2.2. Executing the audit programme

Gathering evidence

Evidence should be gathered on all matters related to audit objectives and scope of work. The IIA proposes several standards to uphold throughout the evidence-gathering process:

- Standards of evidence (Standards 2130, 2310)
- Reliance on the work of others (Standard 2050)
- Developing and recording findings (Standards 2320 and 2330).

Audit teams rely heavily on evidence to support their opinion on whether a criterion is being met. Evidence is considered appropriate if it is sufficient, reliable, relevant, and useful to support conclusions made in relation to the engagement's objectives.

- **Sufficient** information is factual, adequate, and convincing so that a prudent, informed person would reach the same conclusions as the auditor.
- **Reliable** information is the best attainable information through the use of appropriate engagement techniques.

- **Relevant** information supports engagement observations and recommendations and is consistent with the objectives of the engagement.
- **Useful** information helps the organisation meet its goals.

The test of the quality of working papers is whether or not another auditor could take over an engagement and carry on.

When analysing the information and concluding on an objective it is important to note that a single type of evidence is less persuasive than a combination of several types of corroborating evidence. In general, a combination of evidence from different sources and of different types provides a greater degree of credibility than individual items of evidence. A combination of evidence may not always be possible as it is dependent on the subject matter and nature of the issue. The auditor's professional judgement plays a key role in determining if the evidence is a sufficient base for conclusions or findings. Methodologies (or evidence sources) applied to gather evidence for each defined criteria should be well articulated in the audit programme (developed during the planning phase of the audit).

Methods of collecting information

Methods for gathering evidence vary depending on the approach used to conclude on an objective.

Traditional methods for gathering evidence include:

- Physical observation of operations or assets (i.e. walkthrough).
- Auditee packages (i.e. a collection of document requests and technical questions).
- Detailed testing of transactions (i.e. file review).
- System testing.
- Computation or independent validation of calculations.
- Document review and analysis.
- Interviews, focus groups, enquiries and surveys.
- Analysis of information or data (i.e. data analytics, trends, ratio or regression analysis).

During interviews the auditor obtains information from knowledgeable staff within and outside the subject area. It is important for the auditor to hear different perspectives from various roles, geographic locations, and hierarchy/positions when formulating findings.

Developing working papers

Working papers are required to support the substantiation of the engagement objectives and criteria. As per IIA Standard 2330: "Internal auditors must document relevant information to support the conclusions and engagement results." Working papers should be neat, accurate, concise, complete and logical.

The following should be included:

- Interview notes, test results and documentation directly related to findings.
- Referencing of key documents (i.e. policies, procedures, flow charts, etc.).

- Evidence and analysis to support reported observations.
- Significant correspondence with the auditee(s)
- Communications of audit findings and management comments on review results.

The working paper is divided into four sections: analysis, test results, documents summaries, and interview notes. Audit teams should document results under the applicable assessment criteria. The results need to provide evidence and analysis that relates to the cause and its effects/impacts, and articulate conclusions and potential recommendations.

Once analysis of the test results, documents and interviews has been completed, audit analysis summaries must be developed for each audit criteria. Key findings pertaining to an audit criteria should be outlined in an audit analysis tab. Findings should be articulated in a complete and clear manner and should include qualifiers to highlight the degree of confidence that the team has in the finding. Depending on the findings, and nature of the audit, it may be appropriate to have findings documented at a more granular level. As noted previously, corroborating evidence from different sources provides more credibility than an individual item of evidence.

The purpose of articulating consolidated findings from the different tabs is to build and validate audit conclusions and opinions in support of the audit report. It is best practice for these findings to be supported by the assessment of impacts and risks (i.e. between what is and what should be).

In some cases, findings may not be only negative, and there may be activities within the audited entity that can be considered best practice. Highlighting positive observations and good practice in the report, in combination with potentially negative observations, will lead to a balanced report. However, there may be cases where, based on the analysis, a balanced report is not feasible.

6.2.3. Engagement findings debriefs

Formulating the storyline

Prior to debriefing the auditee and developing recommendations, the audit team should reflect on how they will present the observations to management. Using a marketing approach to package the value and importance of the observations will propel management to take action. Bringing together technical observations and horizontal linkages will ensure that the storyline is complete and not perceived as too complex and/or disjointed. A good storyline will catch management's attention and compel them to act.

Formulating recommendations

Developing preliminary recommendations is part of formulating a storyline. Recommendations address identified observations (i.e. risks and exposure) and should be feasible and appropriate. When developing recommendations it is important that the audit team works with the auditee to find a suitable and appropriate solution. One of the best ways that internal audit can add value is to develop recommendations that address the cause of the problem, and not the symptoms. It is vital that the recommendation is addressed to the correct individual who can ensure that it is actioned.

When developing recommendations the audit team should ask the following questions:

- Do they address the risk? Are they realistic?
- Are they cost-effective (i.e. do the benefits/risks outweigh the costs)?
- Does the auditee have the authority, expertise, resources and technology to implement recommendations?
- Do the recommendations fit the auditee's mandate, current operations, future vision/direction, environment and culture?
- Is the recommendation a stop-gap measure, short-term fix or long-term solution?
- Is the recommendation consistent with departmental priorities and objectives?
- If you were accountable for the results, would you implement this recommendation?

While these questions can be hard to assess, they are designed to prompt the audit team to prepare recommendations that will add value to the client and senior management.

Recommendations attributed as meaningful have the following characteristics:

- Clear, succinct, specific and sufficiently detailed to make sense on their own.
- Broadly stated, i.e., stating what needs to be done, while leaving the specifics of how to the management of the audited entity.
- Action-oriented, i.e., presented in the active voice and addressed to the organisation that has the responsibility to act.
- Positive in tone and content.
- Allows for subsequent follow-up to easily determine whether it has been acted upon.
- Coherent and consistent with the other recommendations in the audit report.
- Clearly identifies those responsible for action.

Management letters

If there is a finding of significant importance during an audit, particularly pertaining to imminent systems failure, fraud, corruption, etc., then the auditor should submit these findings directly to management via a management letter. The level of substantiation is much lower than for an audit. Management letters can also be provided to management at the time of the debrief or afterwards for matters of importance that may not be included in the scope of the audit.

Engagement debrief

The purpose of the auditee debrief is to engage the user of the services early in order to review and discuss observations, findings, and potential recommendations. This ensures that all pertinent information has been considered and that the auditee is aware of the observations noted. This on-going engagement is a good opportunity for the user of the services to work with the audit team to help develop effective solutions and recommendations. It also provides an opportunity to identify areas of improvement (i.e. misinterpretations) that were transcribed by the audit team, and allows the audit team to discuss points of interest that are not significant enough for the written engagement report.

The audit team should formally discuss all significant engagement findings and conclusions with the client before the engagement report is drafted. This formal debriefing helps ensure that:

- There are no surprises regarding reporting results.
- There have been no misunderstandings or misinterpretations.
- The audit team is aware of all evidence and corrective action that has already been taken by the auditee.
- Feedback on proposed recommendations is provided by the auditee.

At this time it may also be useful for the audit team to discuss less significant findings that could appear on a management letter or not otherwise be formally reported.

Participants in these debrief sessions should include: individuals who are knowledgeable about the activity being audited, as well as those who can discuss potential corrective actions; senior management responsible for the area being audited; and the audit team leader and any audit team members.

The drafting of the report can be initiated after the findings/observations have been thoroughly discussed with the user of the services.

6.3. Audit reporting

Reporting is the accumulation of the planning and conduct phases of the engagement. In this phase, the audit team formally communicates their observations, along with their opinions and recommendations. They also receive management comments and challenge the management response and proposed action plan.

The final product (i.e. report) is presented to the MAC and then recommended for approval by the secretary general. The report is then shared with the minister and other designated parties:

The ultimate outcome is to produce appropriate, credible, and objective products that can support the organisation achieve its objectives.

Box 6.5. Key activities and outputs for the audit reporting phase

Activities

1. The audit team drafts the audit report and obtains the audit entity's review.
2. After the client's review the report is presented to the MAC and approval of the general secretary is sought.
3. The final approved auditor report should be shared with the minister for their information.

Key outputs

- The audit team should present a draft audit report, management response, and management action plan to the MAC.
- The audit team is responsible for developing the presentation material that they will use to support the tabled report findings.

Box 6.6. International Professional Practice Framework (IPPF): Reporting phase

The Institute of Internal Auditors' Standards for Professional Practice of Internal Auditing outlines the following requirements:

- Internal auditors must communicate results of engagements (Standard 2400).
- Communications must include the engagement's objectives and scope as well as applicable conclusions, recommendations, and action plans (Standard 2410).
- Internal auditors are encouraged to acknowledge satisfactory performance in engagement communications (Standard 2410.A2).
- Communications must be accurate, objective, clear, concise, constructive, complete, and timely (Standard 2420).
- Internal auditors may report that their engagements are "conducted in conformance with the International Standards for the Professional Practice of Internal Auditing" only if the results of the quality assurance and improvement programme support the statement (Standard 2430).

Source: IIA (2016), International Professional Practices Framework, Institute of Internal Auditors.

Figure 6.3. Summary of key activities for the reporting phase

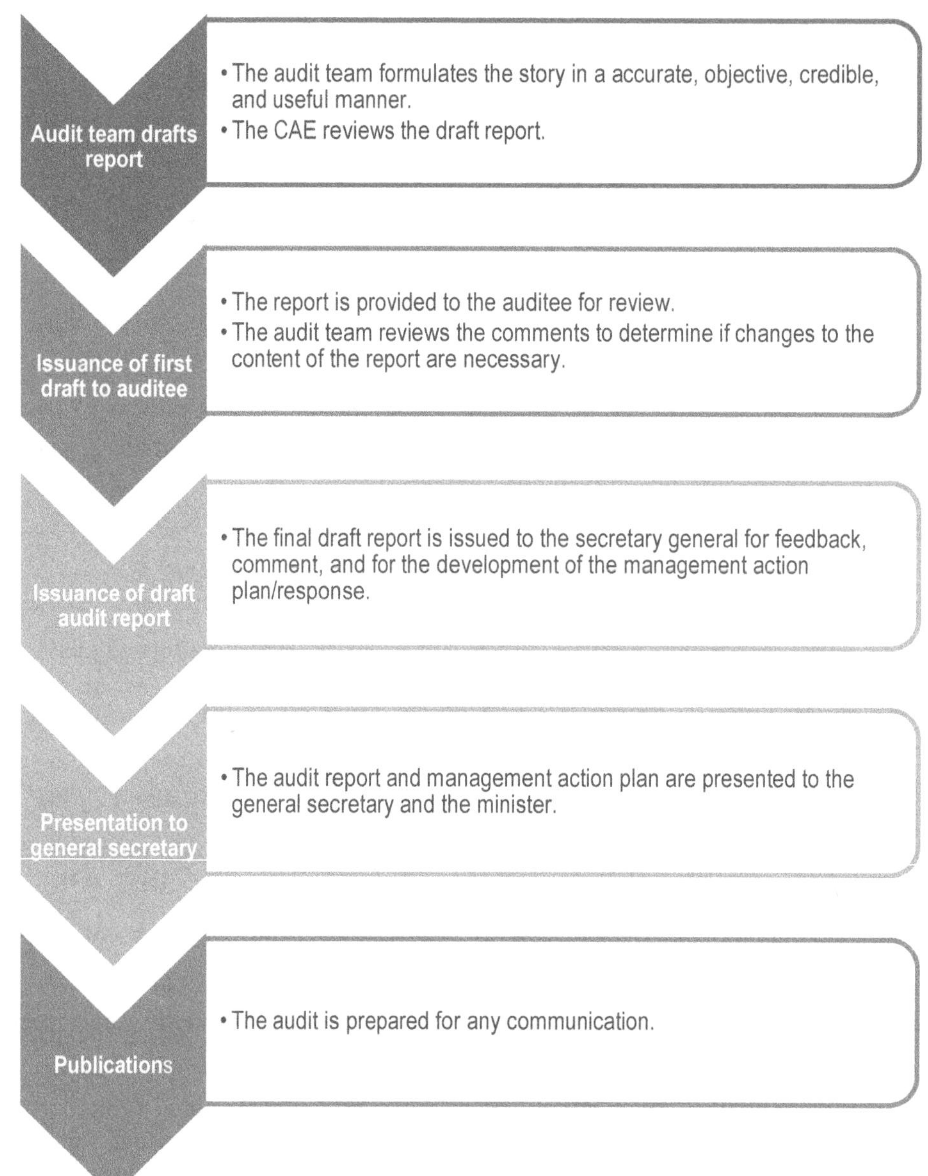

Source: Adapted from: Government of Canada (2016), Audit Manual, Human Resources and Development Canada, Government of Canada.

6.3.1. Audit team drafts audit report

The audit team drafts the audit report after the debrief sessions with the auditee. As noted previously, an open line of communication is essential for forming trust and ensuring that observations and recommendations are well received by the user of the services.

Written reports are the most tangible output of an audit process, and in most cases the key product for the auditee. The audit function is generally valued based on the worth of its findings and the quality of its recommendations. As a result, it is vital that reports are accurate, objective, credible, clear, and useful to management.

The message conveyed in the report is essential for supporting readers' understanding of the issue and the impacts. Audit reports can be written thematically or by lines of inquiry/criteria. When determining how to configure the report, the author should take into consideration the best approach to communicate observations/findings to the user of the services and general public. Audit teams need to be aware that the report is the key instrument for communicating audit results to officials at various levels within the ministry and other government organisations/central agencies.

Features of a good report

Understanding the audience and their needs is the key component of effective report writing. Understanding the environment and business condition will allow the audit team to incorporate observations in the most meaningful way to support the auditees' acceptance and compel them to take action. The following are characteristics of effective report writing:

- **Accurate:** reported observations should be factual and free from errors and distortions. Reports should only include information, findings and conclusions supported by sufficient and appropriate evidence.
- **Objective:** findings should be conveyed with the correct tone that demonstrates objectivity and reasoning. Readers should be left with an impression that the entity was treated fairly. Language that generates defensiveness or opposition should be avoided.

One inaccuracy can cast doubt on the validity of an entire report.

- **Credibility:** reports presented in an unbiased manner will give readers confidence that the observations are objective and that audit results are presented completely and without exaggeration.
- **Clear:** reports should be easily understood and logical. Clarity can be improved by avoiding unnecessary technical language or jargon, and by providing sufficient supporting information.
- **Concise:** reports should be to the point and avoid unnecessary detail.
- **Constructive:** constructive reports help organisations improve. The report should be useful, positive, and aligned to the objectives of the organisation.
- **Complete:** complete reports contain all significant audit results and fully address the objectives outlined in audit terms of reference. Reports contain all relevant information needed to support conclusions and facilitate an adequate and correct understanding of matters reported.
- **Timely:** reports should be issued without undue delay, permitting prompt action.

The auditee should be given approximately two weeks for review of the first draft of the audit report. After receiving the auditee's feedback, the audit team should review the comments to determine if changes to the content of the report are necessary. In some cases, findings noted may conflict with the auditee's opinions, or there might be significant disagreement regarding the presentation of facts. If this occurs, the audit team leader and/or the CAE should discuss these issues with the auditee to determine a suitable course of action.

To facilitate the development of a management response and action plan, the final draft report should be sent to the head of the audited entity with a template outlining the information required for a management response and detailed action plan, as well as a memorandum explaining the request.

The following information should be communicated to the branches:

- Management response: should be short and clear, normally not more than two paragraphs per recommendation. The response should be concise to illustrate whether management agrees with the recommendations.
- If the recommendation is "accepted in part" there should be an explanation as to why corrective action cannot be taken at this time or an explanation/justification as to why the recommendation is only being accepted in part.
- If the recommendation is "rejected" there should be an explanation or justification of why the recommendation is not accepted and, if applicable, an acknowledgement of management's agreement to accept the risk of taking no action. Should significant disagreement exist between auditors and auditees regarding the content of reports and recommendations, the CAE should discuss with the audited entity's management to resolve any impasses. If negotiation is unsuccessful, reports should present the opinions of both auditors and clients to the MAC.
- Management action plan: the action plan should address each recommendation in the audit report individually and provide detailed actions that will be undertaken by management to address the recommendations.

6.3.2. Presentation to senior management

Senior management of the programme or service being audited should review and recommend for approval the internal audit report and corresponding management action by the ministry general secretary. In support of this mandate, it is useful to create a regularly convened meeting of senior management, which can include external members from other organisations, such as GSAC, as well as other representatives from organisations such as the Court of Auditors or inspection bodies. At these meetings the CAE will present internal audit reports. The meetings are also an opportunity for the CAE to communicate any areas where, in his/her opinion, management has accepted a level of risk that is unacceptable to the ministry or to the government.

Senior managers leading the service or programme being audited are expected to appear before the MAC to discuss the results of internal audits conducted, as well as to present the corresponding management action plan that addresses any identified recommendations.

The audit team is responsible for developing the presentation material that will be used to support the tabling of the report.

The approval of reports by the general secretary is sought once the MAC recommends the report for approval. Once approval has been granted, they are deemed complete. They should then be shared with the minister for their information as well as with GSAC.

Information management

The publication process plays an important role in enabling the report to be widely distributed. As part of this process, legal advisors in the ministry should review the audit report to ensure that it respects any privacy or other legal requirements.

Note

[1] In addition to pay-for-service websites where audit programmes can be obtained, internal audit units can collect audit programmes from both within Greece and other EU countries. Other internal audit services are often willing to share any audit programmes developed. Access to free audit programmes can sometimes be found by research on the Internet.

References

Acknowledgements

Relevant standards and definitions from the International Standards for the Professional Practice of Internal Auditing, promulgated by The Institute of Internal Auditors (The IIA), are referenced and included in this guide.

Excerpts from the frameworks established by the Committee of Sponsoring Organizations of the Treadway Commission (COSO): Internal Control - Integrated Framework and Enterprise Risk Management – Integrated Framework are included in this guide.

Audit manuals reviewed

This audit manual includes excerpts from a variety of audit manuals reviewed as part of this project, including:

OECD (2016), A Guide to Planning, Executing and Reporting on Internal Audit Engagements at the Organisation for Economic Co-operation and Development (OECD), Internal Audit and Evaluation Directorate, OECD, Paris (unpublished).

Government of Canada (2016), *Audit Manual*, Human Resources and Development Canada, Government of Canada (unpublished).

Government of Canada (2016), *Audit Manual*, Canadian Border and Security Agency, Government of Canada (unpublished).

Government of Canada (2014), *Internal Audit Reference Centre*, Internal Audit Sector, Office of the Comptroller General, Treasury Board Secretariat, Government of Canada (unpublished).

Ministry of Finance (2013), General Accounting Office, General Directorate for Fiscal Audits, "Standards and Methodologies for Internal Audit Units of Ministries, Decentralised Administrations and other entities".

Ministry of Justice, Transparency and Human Rights, General Secretariat Against Corruption (2016), Operational guidelines for the internal audit units (IAUs).

Other References

Australian National Audit Office (2000), *Benchmarking the Internal Audit Function*, Australian National Audit Office.

Body of Inspectors-Controllers of Public Administration, Koukakis, Maniatis, Souliotis and Selimis (2015), The Internal Audit function in Public Administration.

Cite HR (n.d.), Difference between administrative and functional reporting, www.citehr.com/404301-difference-between-administrative-functional-reporting.html.

COSO (2013), *Internal Control Self-Assessment Checklist, Guidance on Internal Control — Integrated Framework (2013)*, Committee of Sponsoring Organizations of the Treadway Commission.

IIA (2016), International standards for the professional practice of internal auditing (standards), Institute of Internal Auditors.

IIA (2015), International Professional Practices Framework, Institute of Internal Auditors.

IIA (2015), *Creating an Internal Audit Competency Process for the Public Sector*, Institute of Internal Auditors.

IIA (2015), *IPPF Supplemental Guidance: Creating an Internal Audit Competency Process for the Public Sector*, Institute of Internal Auditors.

IIA (2014), *IPPF Practice Guide: Auditing Anti-Bribery and Anti-Corruption Programmes*, Institute of Internal Auditors.

IIA (2013), *Quality Assessment Manual,* Institute of Internal Auditors.

IIA (2012), *IIPF Supplemental Guidance: Implementing a New Internal Audit Function in the Public Sector*, Institute of Internal Auditors.

IIA (2011), *Managing the Business Risk of Fraud: A Practical Guide*, sponsored by the Institute of Internal Auditors, the American Institute of Certified Public Accountants and the Association of Certified Fraud Examiners, Institute of Internal Auditors.

IIA (2009), *IPPF Practice Guide: Internal Auditing and Fraud*, Institute of Internal Auditors.

IIA (2009), *IPPF Supplemental Guidance: Internal Audit Capability Model (IA-CM)*, Institute of Internal Auditors.

Office of the Comptroller General of Canada (2011), *Internal Audit Talent Management, Competency Profiles and Dictionary*, Office of the Comptroller General of Canada.

USAID (2013), *Self-assessment of internal control health sector a toolkit for health sector managers*, United States Agency for International Development.

World Bank (2006), *Keeping an Eye on Subnational Governments: Internal Control and Audit at Local Levels*, Mustafa Baltaci and Serdar Yilmaz Copyright, The International Bank for Reconstruction and Development/The World Bank, Washington, DC.

Glossary

Add value

(Προστιθέμενη αξία)

Internal audit activity adds value to the organisation (and its stakeholders) when it provides objective and relevant assurance, and contributes to the effectiveness and efficiency of governance, risk management and control processes (the IIA Standards Glossary - 2013).

Assurance Services

(Υπηρεσίες διασφάλισης)

An objective examination of evidence for the purpose of providing an independent assessment on governance, risk management and control processes for the organization. Examples may include financial, performance, compliance, system security, and due diligence engagements. (The IIA Standards Glossary - 2013)

Audit committee

An audit committee is comprised of members who are independent from the entity's executive management. It is responsible for the independent review of internal control, risk management and the internal audit function, including monitoring the independence of the internal audit function.

Audit engagement

(Αποστολή Ελέγχου)

A specific internal audit assignment, task, or review activity, such as an internal audit, control self-assessment review, fraud examination, or consultancy. An engagement may include multiple tasks or activities designed to accomplish a specific set of related objectives.

Audit Engagement Opinion

(Γνώμη ελεγκτικής αποστολής)

The rating, conclusion, and/or other description of results of an individual internal audit engagement, relating to those aspects within the objectives and scope of the engagement.

Code of conduct/code of ethics

(Κώδικας δεοντολογίας/κώδικας ηθικής)

Citizens expect public servants to serve the public interest with impartiality, legality, integrity and transparency on a daily basis. Core values guide the judgment of public servants on how to perform their tasks in daily operations. To put these values into effect, organisations establish written, formal codes of behavioural standards. Through a code of ethics (or code of conduct) they can broadly set out the values and principles that define the professional role of public servants (such as integrity, transparency etc., or they can focus on the application of such principles in practice) in conflict-of-interest situations, such as the use of official information and public resources, receiving gifts or benefits, working outside the public service and post public employment. Codes ideally combine aspirational values and more detailed standards on how to put them into practice.

Conflict-of-interest policy (Σύγκρουση συμφερόντων)

A conflict-of-interest policy provides guidance on what constitutes a conflict of interest, how potential conflicts can be managed, and the due processes for resolving a conflict.

Consulting services (Συμβουλευτικέ ς υπηρεσίες)

Advisory and related client service activities, the nature and scope of which are agreed with the client, are intended to add value and improve an organisation's governance, risk management, and control processes, without the internal auditor assuming management responsibility. Examples include counsel, advice, facilitation, and training.

Control processes (Διαδικασίες ελέγχου)

The policies, procedures (both manual and automated) and activities that are part of a control framework and that are designed and operated to ensure that risks are contained within the level that an organisation is willing to accept.

Corruption (Διαφθορά)

Corruption involves efforts to influence and/or the abuse of public authority through the giving or the acceptance of inducement or illegal reward for undue personal or private advantage.

Engagement Work Program (Πρόγραμμα εργασίας αποστολής ελέγχου)

A document that lists the procedures to be followed during an engagement, designed to achieve the engagement plan.

External audit (Εξωτερικός έλεγχος)

External audit is an external and independent activity designed to provide an opinion on the compliance of financial statements with accounting rules and regulations, and if they give a true and fair image of the reality. The certification of financial statements is a legal requirement. In the public sector, external audit is usually performed by supreme audit institutions (SAI).

Forensic Audit

An examination and evaluation of an organisation's or individual's operational, administrative and financial information, in order to collect evidence that could be assessed during a disciplinary and/or criminal procedure.

Fraud (Απάτη)

Fraud involves the deliberate misrepresentation of facts and/or significant information to obtain undue or illegal financial advantage. It may be internal, i.e. originate from within the

	organisation, or external, i.e. involving customers, suppliers, or other third parties.
Governance **(Διακυβέρνηση)**	The combination of processes and structures implemented by the board to inform, direct, manage and monitor the activities of the organisation towards the achievement of its objectives.
IIA **(ΙΕΕ)**	Established in 1941, the Institute of Internal Auditors (IIA) is an international professional association. It is the internal audit profession's global voice, recognised authority, acknowledged leader, chief advocate, and principal educator. Members work in internal auditing, risk management, governance, internal control, information technology audit, education, and security.
Independence of internal audit **(Ανεξαρτησία εσωτερικού ελέγχου)**	The freedom from conditions that threaten objectivity or the appearance of objectivity. Such threats to objectivity must be managed at the individual auditor, engagement, functional, and organisational levels.
Internal audit **(Εσωτερικός έλεγχος)**	Internal auditing is an independent, objective assurance and consulting activity designed to add value and improve an organisation's operations. It helps an organisation accomplish its objectives by bringing a systematic, disciplined approach to evaluate and improve the effectiveness of risk management, control and governance processes.
Internal audit charter **(Κανονισμός Λειτουργίας ή Καταστατικός Χάρτης Εσωτερικού Ελέγχου)**	An internal audit charter is a formal document that defines an activity's purpose, authority and responsibility. It establishes the activity's position within the organisation; authorises access to records, personnel and physical properties relevant to the performance of engagements; and defines the scope of internal audit activities.
Internal control **(Σύστημα Εσωτερικού Ελέγχου)**	Internal control has been broadly defined by the Committee of the Sponsoring Organizations of the Treadway Commission (COSO – www.coso.org) in "Internal Control – Integrated Framework", as: "…a process effected by an entity's management designed to provide reasonable assurance regarding the achievement of objectives in the following categories: • Effectiveness and efficiency of operations; • Reliability of financial reporting; and • Compliance with applicable laws and regulations."

Internal Controls (Δικλίδες εσωτερικού ελέγχου)	A set of procedures and processes put in place by management throughout the administrative, financial and operational functions, in order to tackle the risks threatening the achievement of the organisation's goals and to mitigate the appearance of low productivity and efficiency, as well as mitigate the appearance of fraud or maladministration cases.
INTOSAI (Διεθνής Οργανισμός Ανωτάτων Οργάνων Ελέγχου)	The International Organisation of Supreme Audit Institutions (INTOSAI) is a worldwide association of governmental entities. Its members are the chief financial controller offices of nations. INTOSAI is an autonomous, independent and non-political organisation. It is a non-governmental organisation with special consultative status; it operates as an umbrella organisation for the external government audit community. It has provided an institutionalised framework for supreme audit institutions to promote the development and transfer of knowledge, improve government auditing worldwide, and enhance professional capacities.
Investigation (Έρευνα)	A fraud or corruption investigation consists in evidencing the existence, or not, of a fraud or a case of corruption, based on allegations and suspicions. To achieve this objective, specific procedures are performed to determine whether fraud/corruption occurred, who was involved, the fraud scheme, and losses and consequences. Allegations are expressed based on referrals from witnesses on wrongdoing suspicions or on alerts and red flags identified with detective controls. When a fraud or a case of corruption occurs, evidence is gathered for a legal proceeding.
IPPF, International Professional Practices Framework (Διεθνές Πλαίσιο Επαγγελματικών Πρακτικών)	The International Professional Practices Framework (IPPF) is the conceptual framework that organises the authoritative guidance, either mandatory or strongly recommended, promulgated by the IIA. The IPPF comprises: • The definition of internal auditing • A code of ethics • Internal standards for the professional practice of internal auditing • Position papers, practice guides and practice advisories
Objectivity of internal audit (Αντικειμενικότητα εσωτερικού ελέγχου)	An unbiased mental attitude that allows internal auditors to perform engagements in such a manner that they believe in their work product and that no quality compromises are made. Objectivity requires that internal auditors do not subordinate their judgement on audit matters to others.

Overall opinion **(Συνολική γνώμη)**	An overall opinion is an opinion on the overall adequacy of the organisation's policies, procedures and processes to support governance, risk management, and internal controls. It is generally based on the results of multiple audit engagements.
Risk **(Κίνδυνος)**	The possibility of an event occurring that will have an impact on the achievement of objectives. Risk is measured in terms of impact and likelihood.
Risk management **(Διαχείριση των κινδύνων)**	A process to identify, assess, manage, and control potential events or situations to provide reasonable assurance regarding the achievement of the organisation's objectives.
Whistle blowing	Whistle blowing is where a person raises concern about wrongdoing occurring in an organization. Usually this person would be from that same organization. The revealed misconduct may be classified in many ways; for example, a violation of a law, rule, regulation and/or direct threat to public interest, such a fraud, health/safety violations, and corruption. Whistle blowers may make their allegations internally (for example, to other people within the accused organization) or externally (to regulators, law enforcement agencies, to the media or to groups concerned with the issues).

Annex A. Audit tool 1: Developing an internal audit charter

Purpose

- To aid in the development of a ministry internal audit charter.
- To outline the key elements relating to an internal audit charter.
- To provide guidance on the Institute of Internal Auditors (IIA) internal audit charter in the context of the Greek public administration.

Context

The internal audit charter is a formal document that:

- Defines internal audit activity's purpose, authority, and responsibility.
- Establishes internal audit activity's position within the organisation.
- Authorises access to records, personnel, and physical properties relevant to the performance of engagements.
- Defines the scope of internal audit activities.

The first six elements of the charter, as described below, are compulsory and have uniform content government-wide. Expectations of audit practice may vary across ministries and can have additional sub-elements depending on each ministry's operational requirements.

Guiding principle

Develop and maintain an internal audit charter that provides a foundation for conducting audits within the ministry, and that appropriately describes relevant roles and responsibilities.

Roles and responsibilities:

- **Chief audit executive (CAE).** Periodically assess whether internal audit activity's purpose, authority and responsibility, as defined in the internal audit charter, continue to be adequate to enable the activity to accomplish its objectives.
- **Ministerial audit committee (MAC).** Recommend, and periodically review, a ministry internal charter for the administrative approval of the secretary general, and functional review by the minister.
- **Secretary General (or equivalent in the ministry).** Reaffirm charter.
- **General Secretariat Against Corruption (GSAC).**

- o Issue standards relating to the implementation of internal audit and the responsibility to determine professional standards for internal auditing in Greece.
- o Reaffirm charter.
- o Periodically review guidance.

Guidance (steps/action items):

1. Purpose of the internal audit function

By definition, an internal audit is an independent and objective assurance activity designed to add value and improve a ministry's operations. As such, the audit function's purpose is to provide assurance services. Internal audit helps to improve the ministry's operations and targeted objectives by bringing a systematic, disciplined approach to evaluate and add value to the ministerial processes of:

- effective and efficient risk management
- control frameworks and monitoring their components
- governance and oversight.

Assurance refers to an auditor's professional judgement about the appropriateness of his or her conclusions on risk management, control, and governance. Accordingly, the level of assurance is the level of confidence that auditors have in the appropriateness of their conclusions. As indicated in IIA Standard 1000.A1: "the nature of assurance services provided to the organisation must be defined in the internal audit charter."

2. Mission and scope of the internal audit function

<u>Mission</u>

The internal audit mission must be derived from the definition of internal audit. Writing a mission for the internal audit function needs to use the following baseline concepts:

- The provision of independent and objective assurance.
- Adding value to the ministry.
- Improving an organisation's operations.
- Helping the ministry accomplish its objectives by bringing a systematic, disciplined approach.
- Evaluating and improving the effectiveness of governance, risk management, and control processes.

<u>Scope</u>

The scope of work of the internal audit function is to determine whether the ministry's network of risk management, control and governance processes, as designed and represented by management, is adequate and achieves its intended objectives. The scope should ensure the following:

- Risks are appropriately identified and managed.
- Interaction with the various governance groups occurs as needed.

- Significant financial, managerial and operating information is accurate, reliable and timely.
- Activities and actions comply with policies, standards, procedures and applicable acts and regulations.
- Resources are acquired economically, used efficiently and protected adequately.
- Programmes, plans and objectives are achieved.
- Quality and continuous improvement are fostered in the ministry's control process.
- Significant legislative or regulatory issues impacting the ministry are recognised and addressed properly.

When opportunities for improving management control, sound resource stewardship, and the ministry's image are identified during audits, they will be communicated to the appropriate level of management.

3. Accountability

The CAE is administratively accountable to the secretary general for:

- Preparing an annual written report for the secretary general and the audit committee addressing internal audit's independence, proficiency, performance and results relative to its plan. It should include resource utilisation, lessons learned and influences on future plans.
- Reporting significant issues related to the processes for controlling the ministry's activities, including potential improvements to those processes, and providing information concerning such issues through resolution.
- Providing information periodically on the status and results of the annual audit plan and the sufficiency of internal audit resources.
- Co-ordinating with, and providing oversight of, other assurance control and monitoring functions (risk management, evaluation, compliance, security, legal, ethics, environmental and external audit).

General Secretaries of all departments are responsible for ensuring that GSAC is provided with an annual report of the ministry's IA activities.

4. Independence and objectivity

To enable the independence of the internal audit function, its personnel report to the CAE, who reports administratively to the general secretary and functionally to the minister. The CAE will include a regular report on internal audit personnel as part of his or her reports to the audit committee.

For further details, consult the IIA Standard on independence and objectivity (IIA Standard 1100 – Independence and Objectivity).

5. Responsibility

The CAE is responsible for developing a flexible annual audit plan using an appropriate risk-based methodology. The plan of engagements should include:

- Any risks or control concerns identified by management or external auditors.
- Annual audits that address financial statement reporting and other fundamental controls.
- Selected government-wide sector, thematic or horizontal audits.

6. Authority

The general secretary shall ensure that the CAE and staff of the internal audit function are authorised to:

- Have unrestricted access to all functions, records, property and personnel, and have the right to obtain information and explanations from the ministry's employees and contractors, subject to applicable legislation.
- Attend the meetings or have full and free access to the ministry's audit committee and to the committee chair and vice chair.
- Allocate resources, set frequencies, select subjects, determine scopes of work and apply the techniques required to accomplish audit objectives.
- Obtain the necessary assistance of personnel in units of the ministry where they perform audits, as well as other specialised services from within or outside the ministry.
- Have unimpaired ability to carry out their responsibilities, including reporting findings to the general secretary, to the ministerial audit committee and, as appropriate, to GSAC.

The CAE and internal audit staff are not authorised to:

- Perform any operational duties for the ministry, including performing any internal control activities, as this would impair their ability to assess the effectiveness and efficiency of internal controls in an unbiased manner.
- Initiate or approve accounting transactions external to the internal audit function.
- Direct the activities of any ministerial employee not employed by the internal audit function, unless employees have been appropriately assigned to auditing teams or to otherwise assist internal auditors.
- Be responsible for the investigation of wrongdoing.

7. Standards of audit practice

The internal audit function will meet or exceed the IIA Standards.

Annex B. Audit tool 2: Job descriptions

In this audit tool, three example job descriptions are provided: 1) entry level; 2) auditor/audit manager; and 3) chief audit executive. The CAE is presented based upon the OECD recommendation that current heads of audit be elevated to the role of a senior executive in the ministries.

Job description 1: Entry level audit position

Carries out segments of specific audits to support the work of an assigned audit team in accordance with IIA Standards.

Key activities

- Integrate knowledge of a subject matter discipline (e.g. business administration, human resource management, financial management, information technology) to the application of audit methodologies, recommends approaches required to collect and analyse data, and contributes to the preparation of preliminary audit plans and programmes.
- Carry out segments of audits, analyses and synthesises data gathered, and presents observations for discussions with the audit team.
- Explain and discuss the results of reviews with the IA project leader and/or senior internal auditor to confirm, clarify and ensure their understanding and acceptance of observations raised.
- Prepare narrative and statistical input to audit reports, supporting observations raised, and assists in preparing presentations of results to management.

Skills

a) Intellectual skills

Knowledge of event planning, scheduling and co-ordination, including project management methods, techniques and practices. This knowledge is used to: co-ordinate all logistics for the preparation of meetings; develop and implement internal mechanisms for information collection, organisation, protection, delivery, and preservation of information generated from, or of interest to, the committee; develop internal processes and procedures to ensure the quality and timeliness of secretariat services; respond to questions from meeting participants; ensure that briefing materials and other information on key files are current; administer the flow of information to and from committee members; and contribute to the preparation of reports.

Project management skills are required to establish the annual schedules of meetings and oversee the co-ordination of all logistical arrangements.

Knowledge of the ministry's mandate, corporate objectives, organisation, accountability, governance structure, and decision-making process is required to conduct research.

Knowledge of the laws and policies pertaining to administration within the ministry and central agencies, such as GSAC and the General Accounting Office (Ministry of Finance), (e.g. travel, hospitality, procurement of goods and services and contracting) is required in order to: initiate all aspects of logistical support; identify meeting requirements; negotiate goods and services with private sector companies and follow-up on deliverables; and manage the co-ordination of meeting preparation, including ensuring that the needs and sensitivities of members/guests are properly addressed.

Knowledge of the IIA International Professional Practices Framework (IPPF) to understand the context of the work.

b) Communication skills

Interact with senior executives and their staff to seek clarification of their needs, provide information and respond to questions; communicate with senior officials to obtain their material and seek agreement on meeting deadlines; provide instructions to external contractors and suppliers regarding the provision of products and services for meetings and conferences; and negotiate and explain clearly and in detail what type of services are required, such as catering details, translation, printing and signage specifications, audio-visual, teleconferencing and presentation equipment and services. Writing skills to develop, edit and proofread documents prior to submission to senior executives.

Efforts

a) Intellectual effort

Make decisions/recommendations on: the content of reports, planning documents, recommendations, and approaches.

Identify and synthesise information regarding meetings and recommendations on documentation and presentation material; the details of statements of work and terms and conditions for external contractors and suppliers to meet requirements related to the provision of products and services for meetings; and the need for modifications to internal administrative processes that facilitate the collection, review and analysis of key files.

Analyse information and proactively research and consult at to keep the audit manager informed of any issues arising from communications with members and/or the review of documentation.

b) Physical effort

The work requires activities such as focusing for prolonged periods of time while working on a computer to carry out research and analysis. Frequency for individual activities varies depending on the agenda of the day.

Responsibility

a) Technical resources

Hold custodial responsibility for protected and sensitive files. Custodial responsibilities include: filing, storage (particularly of sensitive and protected documents) and archiving as required.

b) Financial resources

Co-ordinate all contracting and hospitality, commits funds for expenditure and controls, and reports on travel, hospitality and other costs. Verifies that supplier invoices are in accordance with terms and conditions and recommends payment.

c) Human resources

Provide guidance on and explain administrative work practices, procedures and internal processes to new staff, colleagues, and temporary help within own organisation, and follow up to ensure that instructions are understood.

Job description 2: Auditor position

Leads assigned components of the internal audit function (i.e. risk-based audit plans [RBAP], IA operations, quality assurance (QA), methods and corporate reporting).

Note: The internal audit function provides senior management with independent assurance services on the effectiveness and efficiency of programmes, policies and controls, and compliance with government policy requirements, industry standards and laws and regulations. It also provides recommendations to enhance management frameworks, risk management, controls and governance processes.

Key activities

- Contribute to the development of the ministry's multi-year audit plans (RBAP) and to annual operational plans as part of the IA audit management team. Ensure that these plans have a balanced content of audits of high-risk audit entities and compliance audits, and reflect a comprehensive programme and administrative overview of the ministry.
- Manage one or more assigned portions of the audit function (i.e. operations, RBAP, liaison with external auditors, QA, methods and/or corporate planning and reporting); approves multiple simultaneous audit work plans and proposed methodologies; forecast human and financial resources required to achieve objectives; and provide briefings to senior management on progress and issues warranting their attention.
- Review and finalise reports, including validating audit working papers, processes, findings, evidence and conclusions; lead the development of executive-level briefing materials.
- Lead research and analysis of IA audit methodologies and technologies to determine and test their applicability to the function; manage the development and customisation of IA manuals, methodologies, training and other documents/work instruments, and ensure that they are in line with IIA standards.
- Contribute as an IA subject matter expert and oversees the implementation of learning plans for new IA auditors.
- Manage the IA function's contribution to strategic level corporate planning and reporting documents.

- Confer with senior management and liaise extensively with the office of the general secretary to ensure the development of strategic agendas, the recording of decisions, follow-up on decisions and reports on progress.
- Represent the ministry and the CAE at intra and inter-ministry meetings to discuss and arrive at solutions to IA issues; provide input to ministry and/or government-wide proposed initiatives; keep members of the management team informed of results and provide briefings on the potential impact on audit operations.

Skills

Intellectual skills

Knowledge of the principles and theories associated with the internal audit life cycle, including risk assessment, policy development, programme administration and quality management, is required in order to:

- Participate as a member of the IA management team and contribute to the development of RBAPs.
- Manage an assigned portion of the audit function (i.e. operations, RBAP, QA, methods and corporate planning and reporting).
- Lead the development of audit methodologies and technologies, including, but not limited to, risk assessment tools to measure impacts, probabilities and different types of risks facing the ministry.
- Provide expertise in the review and validation of audit working papers, processes, findings, evidence and conclusions.
- Lead project teams involved in multiple simultaneous audits.
- Represent the ministry at external venues to address challenges facing the audit community.

Knowledge of the principles and practices of human, financial and project management is required to lead project teams, establish work plans and goals for multi-disciplinary simultaneous audits, approve work plans and recommended courses of action, and propose human and financial resource needs to meet operational requirements. This knowledge is also used to contribute as an IA subject matter expert to the development and implementation of the IA recruitment and development programme for the branch.

Communications skills are required to deal primarily with senior ministry users of the services and inter-ministerial officials to explain the audit processes, present and defend observations, and make recommendations for remedial action. These skills are also required to respond to requests for advice and consultation, provide authoritative advice and support to the IA principal and/or the CAE, and to represent the ministry/agency at various inter and intra-ministry committees, audits, reviews and workshops to oversee the implementation of learning plans for new IA auditors.

Knowledge of the ministry's and IA's mandate, vision, objectives and priorities, management systems, processes, programme structure, organisational hierarchy, delegation instruments and approval structures is required to consult with ministry representatives to collect data on each auditable entity as part of the risk assessment planning process, and identify and report on the potential risk to the ministry as a whole.

This knowledge is also used to: understand the areas of risk and challenges that may impede the ministry from meeting its business objectives and commitments; contribute to the development of multi-year and annual audit plans; and make risk-managed and cost-effectiveness recommendations to improve the performance and compliance of ministry programmes; help conceptualise and lead the development of ministry audit methodologies and technologies; and manage the development and customisation of IA manuals, methodologies, training and other documents/work instruments.

Knowledge is required of the IIA's International Professional Practices Framework (IPPF) for internal audit, as well as of the expenditure management cycle and planning and accountability regimes of the Government of Greece. This knowledge is used to: identify, analyse and report on the potential risks and challenges for the ministry; provide expertise in the development of the RBAP; establish operational plans for the delivery of multi-dimensional and simultaneous audits; analyse and determine the appropriateness of audit methodologies proposed by project team members; and analyse and ensure that audit reports are based on sound evidence-based observations and recommendations. This knowledge is also used to lead the development of audit methodologies, IA manuals and other technical guidance documents, and oversee the development and training of internal auditors.

Knowledge of government legislative and policy frameworks is required to ensure that programme decisions are efficiently managed in a manner that respects sound stewardship and the highest level of integrity, transparency and accountability.

Knowledge is required of the legislation under which the ministry operates and conducts its activities, as well as administrative legislative requirements, as they apply to specific audit activities. This knowledge is used to understand the authorities and interpret provisions to provide relevant recommendations on audit findings and ensure compliance. These requirements should be incorporated into the development of audit methodologies and technical guidance documents.

Knowledge of new trends and practices from the IIA and IPPF is required to ensure compliance by members of the audit team to these professional standards; analyse and adapt new methodologies and technologies; and share knowledge within the IA functional community.

Professional writing skills are required to review and finalise reports, including validating audit working papers, processes, findings, evidence and conclusions. These documents address sensitive issues and must contain evidence-based recommendations to support senior ministry executive decision making.

Efforts

a) Intellectual effort

Analyse the extent of risks and challenges the ministry faces in delivering its business mandate. Various ministry and external considerations should be incorporated. Conduct regular assessments of potential problem areas within the ministry, ranging from administration (internal management) to policy development and/or programme delivery. Identify the need for and recommend the audit of areas considered high risk, as well as compliance audits, to develop a comprehensive programme and administrative overview of the ministry.

Analyse the RBAP and contribute, as a member of the management team, to the development of operational plans, audit strategies for multiple simultaneous audits based on an assessment of available human and financial resources resources within the ministry as well as other government ministries or external consultants.

Develop audit strategies and audit methodologies and lead the work of multi-disciplinary ministry and inter-ministry teams in the achievement of goals and objectives; recommend project plans, monitor progress and support project staff in the achievement of goals.

Validate audit working papers, processes, findings, evidence and conclusions, and formulate executive level briefings on audit observations that pose a high risk for the general secretary and the ministry, including the development of solutions and remedial actions required by senior management to address observations raised.

Make decisions/recommendations to provide senior management with independent assurance services on the effectiveness and efficiency of programmes, policies and controls and compliance with Greece's legislative regime, industry standards and laws and regulations; contribute to the enhancement of management frameworks, risk management, controls and governance processes.

b) Physical effort

The work requires activities such as focusing for prolonged periods of time while working on a computer to carry out research and analysis. Frequency for individual activities varies depending upon the agenda of the day.

Responsibility

Technical resources

Hold custodial responsibility for protected and sensitive files used during the course of the audit. Custodial responsibilities include storage and application of security practices while files are in the possession of the audit team.

Financial resources

Manage budgetary allocations for concurrent audit projects. Forecasts costs, controls expenditures and recommends payment.

Authorise expenditure for travel, contracting, equipment and other needs, and confirms receipt of goods and services as per contract specifications.

Human resources

Lead project teams, establishes work plans and goals for multi-disciplinary simultaneous audits, approve work plans, recommend courses of action, and propose human and financial resource needs to meet operational requirements.

Lead the work of multi-disciplinary ministry and inter-ministry teams in the achievement of goals and objectives; recommend project plans, monitor progress and support project staff in the achievement of goals.

Manage the work of employees. Leadership activities include leading and/or participating in the recruitment process; establishing roles and responsibilities; assigning work; monitoring and assessing performance; mentoring and coaching; determining and establishing learning plans; and resolving performance issues.

Working conditions

Work in an office environment and uses a computer which involves operating a keyboard and being exposed to glare from a computer screen. Travel regularly to conduct audits, reviews and studies. While the work is normally carried out within an office environment, there is some requirement to conduct field visits involving laboratories, remote sites and other non-traditional office environments.

The work requires working on many complex issues at one time; dealing with demands for expert advice and guidance from ministry units and colleagues; producing reports, briefing notes, and technical interpretative reports for senior management within short time frames. The work also involves establishing alliances and good working relationships within and outside government, and throughout the IA community.

Job description 3: Chief audit executive

General accountability

The chief audit executive (CAE) is accountable for directing and approving the establishment of internal audit plans and priorities and the performance of risk-based internal audits, as necessary, to provide an independent assurance overview report to the general secretary on the adequacy and effectiveness of risk management, control and governance processes within the ministry. As an adjunct to the assurance role, and within their sphere of expertise, the CAE and the internal audit team will also provide advisory services to their organisations and offer solution-oriented recommendations for improving risk management, control and governance processes.

Organisational structure

Note: The number of staff reporting to the CAE will vary depending on the ministry. The organisational structure should reflect the ministry situation.

The CAE is one of several executive positions at the first managerial level that reports to the ministry senior executives (i.e. deputy ministers, heads of agencies, general secretaries, chief executive officers).

Nature and scope

According to IIA standards, the internal audit function provides assurance and advice, independent from line management, on risk management, control and governance processes. Internal audit is a professional, independent appraisal function that provides objective, substantiated conclusions as to how well the organisation's risk management, control and governance processes are designed and working. Internal audit adds value by assessing and making recommendations on the effectiveness of the mechanisms in place to ensure that the organisation achieves its objectives in a way that demonstrates informed, accountable decision making regarding ethics, compliance, risk, economy and efficiency.

The general secretary within the ministry or agency is fully responsible for the adequacy of internal audit coverage, including: ensuring that internal audit capacity is appropriate to the needs of the ministry; establishing an independent ministry audit committee; and appointing a qualified CAE at senior executive level who reports directly to the deputy head.

The CAE is responsible for establishing, leading and directing an internal audit function that operates in accordance with the professional internal auditing standards, as defined by the IIA. He or she is responsible for overseeing and approving the establishment of internal audit policies, procedures and plans, and for setting out the priorities of the internal audit function, consistent with organisational objectives.

The CAE is responsible for ensuring that internal audit plans are based on annual risk assessments and considerate of the input of senior ministry management, the audit committee and GSAC as part of government-wide coverage (e.g. annual audits addressing financial statement reporting). The CAE is responsible for supporting the conduct of, and reporting to, the general secretary on results of externally imposed audits. He or she must: work with external auditors, including the Court of Auditors, GAO, and other investigation and inspection bodies, throughout the conduct of the audit engagement; challenge findings (to ensure the ministry is being treated in a fair and transparent manner); review recommended actions; work with ministry management to establish an appropriate response; and follow up on the implementation of that response.

The CAE is responsible for communicating and obtaining the approval of the general secretary for annual audit plans and for advising the general secretary and the audit committee on resource implications. He or she is also responsible for ensuring that internal audit resources are appropriate, sufficient and effectively deployed to achieve the approved risk-based audit plan and to help provide an annual assurance overview report to the deputy head or audit committee on the adequacy and effectiveness of risk management, control and governance processes within the ministry.

The CAE is responsible for monitoring audit activities, ensuring the timely completion of internal auditing engagements, and ensuring that audit reports are provided to the audit committee with a minimum of delay. As an adjunct to the assurance role, and within their sphere of expertise, the CAE and the internal audit team also provide advisory services to their organisations and offer solution-oriented recommendations for improving risk management, control and governance processes. The CAE, after advising the deputy head, is responsible for informing GSAC of any issue of risk, control or management practice that may be of significance to the government and/or require their involvement.

The CAE is responsible for ensuring the development, implementation and maintenance of a quality assurance and improvement programme that covers all aspects of the internal audit function, continuously monitoring its effectiveness, and identifying the need for and leading the introduction of changes to the audit programme/plan.

The CAE is responsible for developing a human resource plan for the recruitment and retention of internal auditors, for ensuring that internal auditors have the appropriate professional qualifications and skills, and that there are opportunities for sufficient training and development to maintain and develop internal auditing competence and meet IIA standards for internal auditors. As HR manager, the CAE must ensure compliance with HR management regulations, standards and practices.

The CAE is also responsible for implementing modern management, accountability and governance practices, and for overseeing and approving branch input to corporate documents, as well as reviewing them from an audit perspective.

The CAE faces numerous challenges in implementing IIA standards. For example, the need to maintain rigorous objectivity and independence while providing advice to audit subjects on ways of improving risk management, control and governance processes. Challenges also arise in demonstrating the value of internal audit to senior executives, who often view audit as an imposition, and in informing them of the benefits to be realised as a result of implementing legislative requirements regarding internal audit, the objective of which is to strengthen public sector accountability, risk management, resource stewardship and good governance.

The CAE is responsible for establishing and maintaining productive working relationships with GSAC, the external audit community, and colleagues and associates in other ministries and agencies to keep up to date with evolving legislative and policy directions. This ensures the sustainability of a strong, credible internal audit regime that has the confidence of the government, contributes directly to effective risk management, has sound resource stewardship and good governance, and is positioned as a key underpinning of governance within ministries and agencies and across government. The CAE, through his or her participation on inter-ministerial committees and working groups, will contribute to and influence the future of internal audit policies, programmes and practices.

Specific accountabilities

- Provide an annual assurance overview report to general secretary and the audit committee on the effectiveness and adequacy of risk management, control, and governance processes in their ministries, as well as reporting on individual risk-based audits.
- Provide advisory services to senior management and offer solution-oriented recommendations for improving inadequate risk management, control and governance processes identified through the audit function.
- Direct the development, and obtain the general secretary's approval, of risk-based audit plans that consider input from senior management, the audit committee and GSAC.
- Direct and monitor the conduct of internal audit activities, and ensure that audit resources are effectively deployed, audit engagements are completed on time, and reports are provided to the audit committee with a minimum of delay.
- Support, monitor and challenge the results of external audits, reports findings to the general secretary, and work with ministry managers to develop and implement an appropriate response to audit recommendations.
- Interpret audit results and, after discussion with the general secretary, inform GSAC of any issue of risk, control or management practice that may be of significance to the government and/or require their involvement.
- Ensure the development and implementation of a quality assurance and improvement programme covering all aspects of the internal audit function, and, in collaboration with the audit committee and GSAC, ensure that external reviews of the internal audit function are conducted on a periodic basis and the results communicated to the general secretary, the audit committee and GSAC.
- Establish human resource plans and ensure that internal auditors have appropriate professional qualifications and skills to perform audit activities in accordance with the IIA's Professional Practices Framework.
- Function as the ministry internal audit authority regarding its relationship with GSAC, and ensures that ministry interests and concerns are presented and

defended in the development of government-wide internal audit legislation, policies and directives.

- Manage assigned human and financial resources with probity and professionalism, and ensure adherence to modern management principles and practices.

Annex C. Audit tool 3: Control self-assessment worksheet

	Inadequate (-1)	Needs improvement (0)	Adequate (+1)	Comments
1. Control environment				
a. There is a clear set of standards for internal control.				Identify or attach evidence Gap(s) and action: Responsible person: Due date:
b. The standards are based on the regulatory framework.				
c. There is a "code of ethics" that is well publicised and understood by management and staff.				
d. The code of ethics includes requirements of top management and senior staff to disclose gifts, outside interests, personal financial interests, outside positions, and other potential conflicts.				
e. The code of ethics is being followed by staff and includes disclosure by top management and senior staff.				
f. Management and staff exhibit a supportive attitude towards internal control at all times throughout the organisation, including: dedicating qualified full-time staff to this function; issuing, updating, and communicating necessary policies and procedures on a regular basis; and recognising compliance as an element of annual performance.				
g. Management and staff demonstrate a commitment to competence, and training is provided on an ongoing basis to ensure that relevant skills are increased and maintained.				
h. The organisational structure is supportive of a control environment. For instance, it provides assignment of authority and responsibility, empowerment and accountability, and appropriate lines of reporting.				

		Inadequate (-1)	Needs improvement (0)	Adequate (+1)	Comments
i.	Human resources policies and practices are supportive. For instance, recruitment, performance appraisal and promotion processes are based on merit.				
2. Risk assessment					
a.	A formal risk management system is in place and operational.				Identify or attach evidence Gap(s) and action: Responsible person: Due date:
b.	Risks have been identified, assessed, and ranked.				
c.	Internal audit reviews these risks and controls as part of the annual audit programme.				
d.	There is a quarterly review of the risks by line management.				
e.	There is identification of control gaps and implementation of control actions/treatments in response.				
3. Control activities					
a.	In general, control activities occur throughout the organisation, at all levels and in all functions. They include a range of detective and preventive control activities, such as authorisation and approval procedures; segregation of duties (authorising, processing, recording, reviewing); controls over access to resources and records; verifications; reconciliations; reviews of operating performance; reviews of operations, processes, and activities; and supervision (assigning, reviewing and approving, guidance, and training).				Identify or attach evidence Gap(s) and action: Responsible person: Due date:
b.	The ministry has its own financial policies and procedures implementing those of the Ministry of Finance.				
c.	The ministry adheres to Ministry of Finance financial policies and procedures.				
d.	Effective financial accounting systems and controls are in place.				
e.	Actual and planned budgets are compared and differences explained.				

	Inadequate (-1)	Needs improvement (0)	Adequate (+1)	Comments
f. There are reasonable revenue projections in the budget and differences with actual budget are explained.				
g. There is a high degree of stakeholder access to key fiscal information.				
h. There are opportunities for stakeholders to review and comment on budgets before they are finalised.				
i. Policy costs are estimated and forecast properly for future years.				
j. The budget document includes activity statistics and performance information on the effectiveness of existing programmes.				
k. Over/under spending is reported to the ministry's budget office.				
l. Commitments are made consistent with procedures.				
m. Existing rules and procedures for making payments are followed.				
n. An appropriate information management system (FMIS) is in place and functioning.				
o. Access controls limit or detect access to computer resources (data, programmes, equipment, and facilities)				
p. System software controls limit and monitor access to programmes and sensitive files that control the computer hardware and secure applications				
q. Policies, procedures, and an organisational structure are established to ensure segregation of duties.				
4. Information and communication				
a. Transactions and events are recorded promptly when they occur.				Identify or attach evidence Gap(s) and action:
b. Recording covers the entire process or life cycle of a transaction or event.				Responsible person: Due date:

		Inadequate (-1)	Needs improvement (0)	Adequate (+1)	Comments
c.	Information is organised, categorised, and formatted such that reports, schedules, and financial statements can be prepared.				
d.	Information systems produce reports that contain operational, financial and non-financial, and compliance-related information that make it possible to run and control operations.				
e.	Reporting is appropriate, timely, current, accurate, and accessible.				
f.	The internal control system and all transactions and significant events are fully and clearly documented (e.g. flow charts and narratives) and readily available for examination				
g.	Management is kept up to date on performance, developments, risks, and the functioning of internal control and other relevant events and issues.				
h.	Management maintains formal communication mechanisms that provide staff the information they need to implement internal controls, and that provide feedback and direction to staff on internal control weaknesses.				
i.	Management communicates the importance and relevance of effective internal control and the organisation's risk tolerance, and makes personnel aware of their roles and responsibilities in effecting and supporting internal control.				
j.	Management ensures adequate formal and informal means of communication with external parties, including audit bodies, parliament, civil society, and media, to keep them abreast of internal control matters.				
5. Monitoring					
a.	Ongoing monitoring of internal control is a normal part of the operation of the organisation and is performed continually on a real-time basis. It includes regular management and supervisory activities and other actions personnel take in performing their duties.				Identify or attach evidence Gap(s) and action: Responsible Person: Due Date:
b.	Ongoing monitoring activities cover each of the internal control components and involve action against irregular, unethical, uneconomical, inefficient, and ineffective internal control systems.				
c.	The monitoring process reacts dynamically to changing conditions through regular updates to policies and procedures communicated to staff.				

		Inadequate (-1)	Needs improvement (0)	Adequate (+1)	Comments
d.	Decisions on the scope and frequency of separate evaluations (such as this self-assessment) are based primarily on the assessment of risks and the effectiveness of ongoing monitoring procedures.				
e.	When making this determination, the organisation considers: the nature and degree of changes, from both internal and external events, and their associated risks; the competence and experience of the personnel implementing risk responses and related controls; and the results of ongoing monitoring.				
f.	Specific separate evaluations cover the evaluation of the effectiveness of the internal control system and ensure that internal control achieves the desired results.				
g.	All deficiencies found during ongoing monitoring or through separate evaluations are communicated to those positioned to take necessary action.				
h.	Protocols exist to identify what information is needed at a particular level for effective decision making.				
i.	Monitoring internal control includes policies and procedures aimed at ensuring that the findings of audits and other reviews are adequately and promptly resolved.				

Annex D. Audit tool 4: Example communication pamphlet

Background

Mission

The mission of the internal audit function is to provide independent and objective assurance services designed to add value and improve ministry operations. It helps the ministry accomplish its objectives by bringing a systematic, disciplined approach to evaluate and improve the effectiveness of the risk management, internal control and governance frameworks and processes.

Audit practice requirements

To strengthen auditing within ministries, the Government of Greece requires that all ministries possess an internal audit function. Ministries are legally required to meet a set of mandatory requirements, including the Internal Auditing Standards as part of the Institute of Internal Auditors' (IIA) Standards and Code of Ethics.

Ministry audit committee (MAC)

As the lead central agency responsible for internal audit, the General Secretariat Against Corruption requires that all deputy heads of ministries establish and maintain an independent audit committee comprised of senior ministry official and one or two external members from institutions such as the Court of Auditors or an inspections body. This committee provides objective advice and recommendations to the general secretary regarding the sufficiency, quality and results of assurance on the adequacy and functioning of the ministry's risk management, control and governance frameworks and processes (including accountability and auditing systems). The committee typically meets four times a year.

Chief audit executive

The general secretary is also responsible for nominating a qualified chief audit executive (CAE) to the minister. The CAE will report directly to the deputy head and will lead and direct the internal audit function.

Risk-based audit plan

As part of the risk-based audit planning process, the internal audit unit conducts, in collaboration with senior management, an annual ministry-wide risk assessment that includes all functional areas. The purpose of the assessment is to identify, prioritise and schedule audit projects for the following two years, based on areas of higher risk and significance. At the end of this assessment, a risk-based audit plan is drafted and presented to MAC to review and recommend the secretary general's approval and submission to the minister.

While internal audit units carry out audits in accordance with the approved risk-based audit plan, the CAE and internal auditors stay alert to any emerging risks, priorities and/or senior management requests. Status reports are presented to MAC, including a mid-year update in the autumn.

Execution of an audit engagement

There are three phases involved in an internal audit project: planning, conduct and reporting.

Planning phase

The purpose of the planning phase is to gain a good understanding of the audit entity, including its management and business processes and practices, policies and procedures, and external and internal environment. In this phase, auditors review key documents, conduct preliminary interviews, and perform a detailed risk assessment of the audit entity to confirm the audit objective and determine the key areas that warrant further examination.

The audit plan (or terms of reference) is drafted at the end of the planning phase. It describes the audit entity, objective, scope, criteria and timeframes, as well as the approach used to assess selected areas against the audit criteria. A summary of this plan is provided to audit entity management to obtain their agreement on the established audit criteria, and to keep them informed of the results of the planning activities and the timeframes of the audit.

Conduct phase

Once the audit plan is approved by the CAE, the audit team conducts the audit following the approach outlined in the plan. At this stage, auditors review all key documents, conduct additional interviews, test key controls and gather and analyse data from various sources. At the end of this phase, auditors provide a formal debriefing on the findings to audit entity management. During the debriefing, management is invited to make comments, provide feedback and/or confirm the factual accuracy of findings for auditors to consider before completing the detailed audit work and starting the writing of the audit report.

Reporting phase

During the reporting phase, auditors draft an audit report which includes findings and recommendations, when actions are considered necessary. This report is submitted to audit entity management for validation of the content, including the findings. A formal management response, including an action plan when deemed appropriate, is requested by the CAE. The action plan is assessed by auditors, integrated into the draft audit report, and presented to the MAC for review and recommendation. Senior management is asked to attend a meeting to discuss the content of the draft audit report with MAC members. Following recommendation by MAC, the draft audit report is submitted to the deputy head for approval prior to submission to the minister.

Management action plan (MAP)

The internal audit unit undertakes an annual exercise at the conclusion of each fiscal year to request a status update for all outstanding MAPs that respond to both internal and external audit recommendations. For all completed actions, supporting documentation is requested to enable the internal audit unit to conclude its verification process. Results and identified residual risks are subsequently reported to the MAC and senior management.

Other considerations

Access to ministerial information

IIA standards require that the general secretary provides the CAE with access to all ministerial records, databases, workplaces and employees, and allows them the authority, within the context of carrying out audit projects, to obtain information and explanations from ministerial employees and contractors.

Confidentiality of audit records

The CAE controls access to all project records. Although requests for access to records from external parties are rare, the CAE consults with senior management or legal advice prior to releasing audit records to external parties.

Annex E. Audit tool 5: Example audit universe

What is an auditable activity?

Risk-based auditing (RBA) occurs at the macro-level (annual audit planning) and the micro-level (conducting an audit). Determining "auditable units" or activities is one of most important parts of RBA, but no "best practice" or IIA Standard on how to carry this out exists. Some possibilities are:

- By organisational unit or location
- By function, process or business cycle
- By major IT applications
- By lines of business or major programmes/contracts
- By affiliated/subsidiary agencies
- Combinations of the above

Many, if not most, large audit groups (more than 15 auditors) have multiple annual audit plans, each with different ways of determining auditable activities.

Level 1 (Activity cluster)	Level 2 (Line of business)	Level 3 (Business segment/Programme)
Management framework	Ministerial governance	Organisational structure
		Governance committees
	Delegation of authorities	Delegation of authorities – finance & HR
	Ministerial frameworks	Internal control (policy on internal controls)
		Grants and contributions (i.e. financial transfers)
		Fraud
		Privacy (PIC)
		Security
	Value and ethics management	Internal disclosure/whistleblowers
		Code of conduct
		Conflict of interest and post-employment
Planning & accountability	Planning and risk management	Integrated planning and risk management
		Investment planning (including costing)
		Financial planning (including costing, budgeting, allocating, forecasting, tracking, coding)
		Workforce planning
		IT planning (including costing)
		Emergency management planning
		Business continuity planning
	Performance measurement and reporting	Financial reporting
		Ministerial financial statements
		Ministerial accountability reporting to parliament (planning and results)
		Human resources reporting
		Reports to parliamentary officers and external auditors
		Proactive disclosure
		Management accountability reporting to central agencies
	Project management & oversight	Major transformation projects and initiatives
	Submissions to central agencies	Requests for funding (e.g. new programmes and services)
	Internal audit	
Asset and resource management	Financial accounting operations	Accounts payable
		Procurement and contracting

Level 1 (Activity cluster)	Level 2 (Line of business)	Level 3 (Business segment/Programme)
		Hospitality
		Travel
		Staff relocation
		Management of contracts (including security)
		Vendor master data - goods and services
		Grants and contributions; salaries for employees
		Accounts receivable revenues; cash management
		Payroll
	Information assets & data lifecycle	Personal information management
		Privacy impact assessments
		Business information management
		Intellectual property
	Tangible and non-tangible assets	Capital lease
		Non-tangible IT assets (software and solutions)
		Accommodations
		Shuttle and fleet
		Tangible IT assets lifecycle and refresh (e.g. desktops, portable digital devices, printers, scanners, facsimiles, telecom and VOIP audio and video conferencing)
Human capital management	Talent recruitment	Organisational design
		Classification
		Staffing
		Employment equity
		Relocation
	Talent management and retention	Talent management
		Learning management
		Pride and recognition
		Employee performance management
	Employee and manager support	Employee assistance services
		Disability management
		Labour relations
		Duty to accommodate
		Alternative work arrangements and telework

Level 1 (Activity cluster)	Level 2 (Line of business)	Level 3 (Business segment/Programme)
		Compensation and benefit including absence and overtime management
		Occupational health and safety
Safeguarding of assets, information and people	Employee identity and access management	Separation clearance
		Privileged access
	Information technology security	Management safeguards
		Technical safeguards
		Operational safeguards
	Physical security (workplace)	
	Contracting security (access, clearance)	
	Personnel security (clearance)	
	Security incidents (including emergency incidents)	
Management of information technology	IT solutions development and acquisition	
	IT solutions operations management	
	IT solutions maintenance	
	End-user support	
	Web standards	
Legal services	Litigation support and dispute resolution	
	Legal advice and litigation services	
	Legal issues management committee	
Communications	Advertising and marketing	
	Internal communications	
	Ministerial website	
	Media Relations (including ministerial events)	
	Strategic communications planning and advice	
	Publications	
	Translation and editing	
	Public consultations	
	Public opinion research	
External relations	Intergovernmental and international relations	Intergovernmental meetings and study tours
		Intergovernmental correspondence
	Service delivery partnerships and business agreements with other government ministries	

Level 1 (Activity cluster)	Level 2 (Line of business)	Level 3 (Business segment/Programme)
	International, intergovernmental and interministerial committees	International (OECD, UN, World Bank, IMF, EU, etc...)
		Inter-ministerial
	Ministerial and executive correspondence	
	Parliamentary affairs	
Policy - programme - services continuum	Management of corporate services with other ministries	Examples could include: procurement, contracting, payroll; web presence
	Research Planning and Management (incl. E-Scanning, Policy Diagnostics)	
	Data, knowledge and analytics	Administrative data
		Open data
	Strategic policy (social development, economic, learning)	Central agency submissions
		Federal budget submissions
		Strategic policy frameworks (including policy planning)
		Regulatory changes
	Medium term policy (including policy planning)	
	Strategy and co-ordination	Submissions to central agencies (e.g. Red Tape)
		Medium term policy and research planning
	Programme and service design	Business plans, (e.g. accuracy of design and costing)

Source: Audit Universe: Adapted from: Government of Canada (2016), Audit Manual, Human Resources and Development Canada, Government of Canada.

Annex F. Audit tool 6: Example risk collection and assessment tool

INSTRUCTIONS: This risk profile should be filled out for each audit entity as part of preparing the risk-based audit plan. The risk assessment grid at the end of this profile provides definitions of risk and should be used to fill out this form. This profile, as well as the risk assessment grid, are provided as examples only and can be modified as required since each organisation's risk exposure and tolerance is different and unique.

Section 1: Entity profile	
Entity name	
Service delivery model	Direct delivery, using third parties, etc.
Background/ Mandate	
FTEs	Full time equivalents (i.e. number of personnel)
Budget	
Volumetric data	(i.e. data sources available to describe the organisation)
Key performance indicators (KPIs)	
Enabling technology/IMIT	
Enabling policy/ legislation	

Section 2: Entity analysis
Relevant past audits (internal, external – within the last 2-4 years)
Name, date
Links
Key issues, findings
Governance – risk – control considerations
Governance
Risk management
Control environment
Control objectives

Section 3: Risk analysis				
Risks: (F: Financial; H: Harm to People; S: Service disruption)[1] ***(Note: See risk assessment grid below for definitions)***	***Likelihood***	***Impact*** F	H	S
Risk analysis				

Note: 1. Add the risk of fraud.

Section 4 : Possible nature of audit engagement/focus (G-R-C)				
Nature				
Focus (G-R-C)				
Rationale				
Estimated start				
Estimated resources	***FTEs***	***Professional services***	***Travel***	***Translation***

Risk assessment grid

		Insignificant	Minor	Moderate	Major	Extreme	Definitions of impact types
Impact types	***Financial Loss (Financial amounts are relative to each organisation and are provided for example purposes only)***	up to 100K Euros	100K - 1M Euros	1M - 50M Euros	50M - 335M Euros	Significant mis-statements on the financial statements.	Non-recoverable financial losses (write-offs) attributed to errors, omissions, fraud, and abuse.
	Harm to individuals	Inconvenience, e.g. closure, strike.	Short-term injury or little financial impact, e.g. data losses.	Long-term injury or financial harm.	Severe or prolonged injury or major financial harm.	Fatalities or genuine risk of death.	Harm to individuals can be in the form of personal injury, inconvenience (loss of personal information) or resulting in financial losses.
	Service disruption to clients	Internal operations do not meet performance targets.	Service delivery does not meet targets but corrected quickly, e.g. website down.	Service delivery compromised beyond the recovery time objective.	Service level falls below minimum and affects all clients in a programme or region.	Services cannot be delivered. Catastrophic failure.	Mission critical operations.
Cascading impacts	***Expected results of programmes or services offering are compromised***	Programme or service offering is subject to internal review with no changes to the programme.	Programme or service offering is strengthened to improve performance.	Programme or service offering is completely redesigned.	Programme or service offering is significantly downsized.	Programme or service offering terminated and removed from organisation mandate.	Expected results impacts are a result of other risk events occurring and their associated impacts. i.e. financial mismanagement, harm to individuals or service disruptions.
	Reputation	Complaints dealt with through regular business processes, e.g. letter to organisational head, minister, complaints re: government service.	Local media attention or special interest stories. Media lines required.	Public trust/ confidence in programme or service is affected. Subject to questions in Parliament.	Loss of public trust and confidence. Sustained national media attention.	Loss of public trust and confidence in the government. Political upheaval. Change in government.	Reputational impacts are a result of other risk events occurring and their associated impacts, i.e. financial mismanagement, harm to individuals or service disruptions.

	Legal	Legal impacts attributed to non-compliance to legislation, regulations and central agency policies and civil jurisprudence, and potentially resulting in legal actions and possible financial settlements.					Legal impacts resulting from external events and their associated impacts, i.e. financial mismanagement, harm to individuals or service disruptions. Legal services' risk assessment methodology focusses on the strength of a legal position if challenged in court.
	Shift in management focus (internally)	Overtime required; handled within existing operations.	Re-allocation of resources limited to the operational area, e.g. postal strike.	Re-allocation of resources across operational areas.	Significant and prolonged mobilisation of department resources affecting normal operations.	Mobilisation of ministry resources to address and significant ministerial, parliamentary and senior management attention.	Shifts in management focus impacts are a result of other risk events occurring and their associated impacts, i.e. financial mismanagement, harm to individuals, service disruptions.

			1	**2**	**3**	**4**	**5**
Likelihood probability	Control failure or targets not met >20% of instances	**5**	5	10	15	20	25
	Control failure or targets not met 10-20% of instances	**4**	4	8	12	16	20
	Control failure or targets not met 5-10% of instances	**3**	3	6	9	12	15
	Control failure or targets not met 2.5-5% of instances	**2**	2	4	6	8	10
	Control failure or targets not met <2.5% instances	**1**	1	2	3	4	5

Annex G. Audit tool 7: Fraud risk assessment guidance tool to assess ministry-wide fraud risk

Assessing ministry fraud awareness and prevention capabilities

Since fraud can occur at any level of an organisation, the ministry must establish appropriate strategies and programmes for fraud awareness and prevention. As part of the fraud risk assessment, the CAE should evaluate the ministry's fraud risk management and prevention activities, including fraud awareness programmes, employee training, communications, and ministry policies and procedures on fraudulent activities.

An effective fraud risk management programme includes a variety of activities, such as:

- A code of conduct and ethics programme that sets the tone at the top.
- A fraud awareness programme to ensure that all employees understand the nature, causes, and signs of fraud, and know what to do if they suspect an act of fraud has occurred.
- A fraud risk assessment that evaluates the risk of various types of fraud.
- Appropriate processes and controls.
- A fraud prevention programme and a fraud response plan.

Activities such as fraud awareness programmes form part of the control environment and can reduce the likelihood of fraud occurring; however, it is important to recognise that the risk of fraud can never be eliminated. There are always individuals, inside or outside the ministry, who are motivated to commit fraud. It would not be cost-effective to try to eliminate all fraudulent activities; instead, internal controls should be designed to detect and minimise fraud risks. Good awareness programmes and internal controls can reduce the opportunities for fraud. By creating a fraud-resistant culture, ministries can avoid not only monetary losses, but also negative side effects, such as adverse publicity, poor employee morale, and lack of public confidence.

The CAE can contribute to a reduction in fraud risk by ensuring that adequate fraud risk management strategies are in place to discourage fraud and to minimise losses should it occur.

Initial fraud prevention activities should include management setting the proper tone at the top, encouraging all employees to exhibit ethical behaviour, and ensuring that everyone understands their responsibilities. A fraud awareness programme will demonstrate to all employees that fraud is a serious issue and will educate them about what to do when faced with possible fraudulent activities.

Assessing the ministry's fraud risk exposure

As part of the CAE's mandate for providing assurance on governance, risk management, and control in the ministry, the CAE must evaluate the potential for fraud and assess how the ministry manages fraud risk. Although the assessment of fraud risk should be an ongoing activity, the annual risk-based internal audit planning process should also include specific activities for assessing fraud risk. Assessments should examine the extent to which:

- Fraud-related ministry mandates, roles, and responsibilities are clear, i.e., what investigative procedures are followed when fraud is detected and who is responsible for their initiation and conduct.
- Disclosure mechanisms under the PSDPA are in place and have been communicated to all employees.
- Established processes and procedures for examining potential acts of fraud are followed;
- concerned ministry officials are suitably involved in these processes.
- Decisions and corrective actions resulting from these investigations have been reviewed by the appropriate bodies.
- Actions taken during, and as a result of, these investigations comply with related legislation and policies.
- These investigations and related activities are reported as required, internally and externally.

The CAE could also review previous acts, allegations, and investigations of fraud to determine if there are systemic issues or control weaknesses that might increase the risk of fraud.

In addition, internal auditors should consider the various factors that either increase the pressure or present opportunities to commit fraud. Table A G.1 presents examples of fraud risks that, when present, can increase the likelihood of fraud occurring. While the presence of a risk factor does not mean that an act of fraud has occurred or will occur, almost all frauds include the presence of one or more of the risk factors, and internal auditors should consider these factors when conducting a fraud risk assessment.

Table A G.1. Examples of risk factors that can increase the likelihood of fraud

Risk factor	Warning signs	Issue
Management environment	Management's own commitment to ethical behaviour is not evident.	An employee who is inclined to commit fraud may feel that he/she is doing something that management would condone or even do itself.
Competitive and business environment	Unethical business practices are accepted among others who operate within the organisation's environment.	An employee who is inclined to commit fraud may feel that he/she is doing something that others in the organisation's environment would do themselves.
Employee relationships	Conflicts of interest and favouritism are accepted within the organisation.	An employee who is inclined to commit fraud may feel that this is an accepted practice.
Attractive assets	Attractive assets are not appropriately controlled.	An employee who is inclined to commit fraud is provided with opportunity.
Technology	Technology is not appropriately controlled.	An employee who is inclined to commit fraud is provided with opportunity.
Lack of segregation of duties	Access to assets and access to the means of concealment are combined.	An employee who is inclined to commit fraud is provided with opportunity.
Insufficient monitoring and control	There is diminished ability to detect wrongdoing.	An employee who is inclined to commit fraud is provided with opportunity for concealing the fraud.

Assessing fraud risk exposure in the course of an internal audit

During the planning of an internal audit engagement, the CAE must consider the potential for fraud. During the conduct of the audit engagement, internal auditors should dedicate adequate time to evaluating the design and operation of internal controls for fraud risk management. As part of regular audit work, internal auditors should exercise professional scepticism when reviewing activities, and be able to recognise the signs of fraud.

Although internal auditors may not know the exact series of events and circumstances that would lead to fraud, they are expected to help the organisation prevent fraud. The CAE should ensure that internal auditors understand the three factors motivating individuals to commit fraud:

1. **Pressure.** The need that an individual attempts to satisfy by committing fraud, e.g. unreasonable deadlines or performance expectations, the need to keep one's job, and financial pressures.
2. **Opportunity.** The belief that an act of fraud can be committed and remain undetected. The opportunity is often reflective of the control environment. Weak controls, poor management, absence of procedures, abuse of authority, and lack of oversight can increase opportunities.
3. **Rationalisation.** The ability to justify the fraudulent act. Fraud perpetrators may believe that they are owed or deserve the gain derived from the fraud, e.g. compensation for unpaid overtime or unfair treatment.

Of these three factors, internal auditors can have the greatest impact on the opportunities to commit fraud. In particular, the development of preventive and detective controls can reduce the risk of someone committing fraud and it going undetected. By addressing the opportunities for fraud, internal auditors can reduce the likelihood that employees will succumb to pressures to commit fraud and then rationalise their actions.

Fraud risk assessment requires a level of reasoning that involves anticipating how the potential perpetrator of fraud may take advantage of opportunities. It also involves designing fraud detection procedures that a perpetrator may not expect. These activities require a sceptical mindset and involve asking the following questions:

- How might a fraud perpetrator exploit weaknesses in the ministry's system of controls?
- How could a perpetrator override or circumvent controls?
- What could a perpetrator do to conceal the fraud?

Such thinking requires internal auditors to have a good understanding of the activities and operations of the audit entity. A fraud risk assessment generally includes three essential elements, although they vary considerably by ministry:

1. Identifying the organisation's inherent fraud risk.
2. Assessing the likelihood and significance of inherent fraud.
3. Responding to reasonably likely and significant fraud risks, both inherent and residual.

Internal auditors should also be alert to signs of fraud in their ministry and, when those signs exist, should consciously decide what additional action is necessary.

Assessing the ministry's fraud detection and investigation capabilities

The CAE should assess the adequacy of the ministry's fraud detection and investigation capabilities. This includes ensuring that the ministry has controls in place to address the risk of fraud and enhance the effectiveness of the ministry's fraud risk management programme. Having effective detective controls in place is a strong deterrent of fraudulent behaviour.

The CAE should also ensure that there are policies and procedures to govern the conduct and reporting of fraud investigations. The mandate and authority to undertake activities relating to the detection, investigation, and reporting of fraud should be explicitly stated in the ministry's fraud policy and procedures. The CAE should ensure that the fraud policy includes a statement setting out expectations for, and the roles and responsibilities of, the principals involved. It should also clearly assign the authority to access documents, records, employees, and senior management in the performance of fraud investigations.

Developing capacity within internal audit to recognise the signs of fraud

Senior management must recognise that internal auditors do not necessarily have all the knowledge and skills of a professional whose primary responsibility is detecting and investigating fraud. Forensic work should be performed by specialists, as contamination of evidence could hinder the ability to proceed with a forensic or police investigation. However, during the conduct of an internal audit engagement, the internal auditor, with a solid analytical background, due diligence, and professional scepticism, should be able to identify the "red flags," or warning signs, typically associated with fraud.

While internal auditors are not responsible for the deterrence, detection, and investigation of fraud, IIA standards contain specific requirements related to fraud:

- **Proficiency**. Internal auditors must have sufficient knowledge to evaluate the risk of fraud and how it is managed by the organisation; however, they are not expected to have the expertise of an individual whose primary responsibility is detecting and investigating fraud.

- **Professional care**. Internal auditors must exercise due professional care by considering the probability of significant errors, fraud, or non-compliance.
- **Reporting to senior management**. Reporting must include significant risk exposures and control issues, fraud risks, governance issues, and other information needed or requested by senior management.
- **Risk management**. The internal audit activity must evaluate the potential for fraud and assess how the organisation manages fraud risk.
- **Engagement objectives**. Internal auditors must consider the probability of significant errors, fraud, non-compliance, and other exposures when developing the engagement objectives.

Though not all acts of fraud can be prevented, early detection and quick, appropriate action can reduce losses. According to the IIA standards, internal auditors must have sufficient knowledge to evaluate the risk of fraud and the manner in which it is managed by the organisation. Accordingly, the CAE must ensure that internal auditors can recognise the signs of fraud. Specific knowledge required includes the following:

- A detailed understanding of the operations and activities of the ministry.
- A detailed understanding of the ministry's functional areas, such as procurement, finance, HR management, and security.
- An understanding of the applicable legislation.
- Knowledge of policies, rules, and regulations.

Specific skills are required to evaluate the risk of fraud, including those typically associated with the internal audit function. These include the following:

- Strong interviewing skills.
- Strong quantitative analysis abilities.
- A good understanding of accounting techniques.
- A strong ability to understand processes and their interactions in a larger ministry and inter-ministerial context.
- A good understanding of information management and information technology.

Accordingly, the CAE must establish and maintain a capacity for evaluating the risk of fraud and for understanding the ministry's significant fraud risk exposures and its management of those risks. Internal auditors should assess fraud risk during the risk-based planning process, as well as consider the risk of fraud during the planning phase of every audit.

On detecting fraud during an internal audit engagement

The CAE needs to ensure that the roles and responsibilities for fraud investigation are clearly understood and communicated. All ministry internal auditors need to know how to proceed when they detect a possible act of fraud or learn of an allegation of fraud. Upon discovering a possible fraud, or being informed of an allegation of fraud, internal auditors should determine if the incident is a control issue, an administrative matter, a wrongdoing, or possible fraud.

Typically, at the beginning of an internal audit, there is an assumption of probable propriety and normal audit procedures are performed. If red flags are noted during the course of the audit, the assumption is one of possible impropriety. Additional testing is performed to verify the existence and meaning of the red flags. If additional warning signs appear, the situation becomes one of possible fraud. If more in-depth testing and analysis continue to give rise to concerns, the situation becomes one of probable fraud. At this point, any additional work must be performed as an investigation, not an internal audit.

The CAE should be informed of any audit that has gone from probable propriety to possible impropriety. If the situation is shown to be a case of possible fraud, the CAE must ensure that any further work is carried out by someone with the skills required to determine whether the situation is a probable fraud or not. If the incident is of a more serious nature, the CAE should determine the appropriate authority to perform additional examination of the probable fraud.

The CAE should also ensure that internal auditors are aware of the roles of other positions with fraud-related responsibilities, such as the ethics advisor, disclosure officer, integrity officer, and the security officer. In particular, policies, procedures, and practices should be in place to:

- Ensure that internal auditors inform the CAE of all alleged acts of fraud.
- Guide the internal auditor's actions when a potential act of fraud is uncovered during an audit.

When an internal audit engagement detects potential fraud (and, to a certain extent, other types of wrongdoing), the CAE should immediately:

- Ensure that any further audit activity does not contaminate possible evidence.
- Ensure that the rights of all involved parties are protected.
- Record and safeguard the audit work completed up to that time.
- Contact the ministry senior executive responsible for undertaking fraud investigations.
- Ensure that there is an orderly transfer of the audit evidence to the responsible senior executive.
- Determine the extent of internal audit's further involvement, e.g. gathering additional background information.

It is important for the CAE to understand that fraud investigations are not simply the extension of audit practices and procedures; they require specialised skills, tools, and procedures. The purpose of a fraud investigation is not to make recommendations on the controls, but to conclude on the evidence. If the responsibility for fraud investigations is assigned to the CAE, it should be treated as separate and distinct from his or her internal audit role.

Appendix: Sample tool for assigning roles and responsibilities

This table is a sample tool for assigning roles and responsibilities and is intended to help ensure that all required activities are addressed, that roles and responsibilities are understood and communicated, and that duplication of effort is minimised when addressing possible fraud.

Action required	Investigation body	Internal auditing	Finance accounting	Management
1. Fraud education and training				P
2. Ethics advice line	S	S		P
3. Incident reporting hotline	S	S		P
4. Controls to prevent fraud	S	S	SR	SR
5. Recommendations to prevent fraud	SR	SR	S	S
6. Proactive fraud auditing	S	P		
7. Risk analysis of areas of vulnerability		SR	SR	SR
8. Investigation of fraud	P	S		
9. Internal control reviews		P	S	S
10. Referrals to law enforcement	P			S
11. Civil litigation	S			P
12. Reporting of results	SR	SR	SR	SR
13. Post-case analysis	SR	SR		
14. Corrective action and recommendations to prevent recurrences	S	S	SR	SR
15. Recovery of monies due to fraud			P	
16. Monitoring of recoveries			P	S
17. Publicity or press releases	S			P

Note: **Legend:** P = Primary responsibility S = Secondary responsibility SR = Shared responsibility

Annex H. Audit tool 8: Fraud risk questionnaire to be used when undertaking an audit engagement

Project title/ Number		Date completed		*Month, day, year*
Fraud planning	**Completed**	**Date**	**Initial**	**Comments**
IA team has sufficient knowledge to evaluate the risk of fraud and how it is managed for the area being examined.	☐			
Fraud risks were discussed during kick-off meeting and/or preliminary interviews.	☐			
The probability of significant errors, fraud, and non-compliance were considered for the area examined.	☐			
Any significant risk exposures and control issues, including fraud risks, have been documented and reported.	☐			
IA team has evaluated the potential for fraud in the area examined (brainstorming session recommended).	☐			
IA team has evaluated the management of fraud within the area examined in terms of preventative and detective controls.	☐			
All areas where the likelihood and impact of significant errors, fraud, noncompliance and/or wrongdoing have been documented and incorporated into the audit/work programme.	☐			
Name: ____________________ Date: __________ Signature: Auditor				

Schedule 1 to the internal audit fraud questionnaire: Assessment of the probability of fraud

1) Have any past internal/external audits or management reviews found occurrences of fraud in the area/programme/process being assessed?

If yes, has management taken action to prevent occurrences of fraud?

2) Based on the information available and the knowledge of the audit team, what types of fraud, if any, could occur in the area/programme/process being assessed (any source to consult for ideas on fraud indicators/red flags)?

For each identified type of potential fraud, answer the questions below:

Identified potential fraud #1

Who could perpetrate the fraud?

Why could this fraud occur?

How could this fraud occur?

When could this fraud occur?

Where could this fraud occur?

What is the probability that this fraud could occur?	
Identified Potential Fraud # ...	
Who could perpetrate the fraud?	
Why could this fraud occur?	
How could this fraud occur?	
When could this fraud occur?	
Where could this fraud occur?	
What is the probability that this fraud could occur?	

ORGANISATION FOR ECONOMIC CO-OPERATION AND DEVELOPMENT

The OECD is a unique forum where governments work together to address the economic, social and environmental challenges of globalisation. The OECD is also at the forefront of efforts to understand and to help governments respond to new developments and concerns, such as corporate governance, the information economy and the challenges of an ageing population. The Organisation provides a setting where governments can compare policy experiences, seek answers to common problems, identify good practice and work to co-ordinate domestic and international policies.

The OECD member countries are: Australia, Austria, Belgium, Canada, Chile, the Czech Republic, Denmark, Estonia, Finland, France, Germany, Greece, Hungary, Iceland, Ireland, Israel, Italy, Japan, Korea, Latvia, Lithuania, Luxembourg, Mexico, the Netherlands, New Zealand, Norway, Poland, Portugal, the Slovak Republic, Slovenia, Spain, Sweden, Switzerland, Turkey, the United Kingdom and the United States. The European Union takes part in the work of the OECD.

OECD Publishing disseminates widely the results of the Organisation's statistics gathering and research on economic, social and environmental issues, as well as the conventions, guidelines and standards agreed by its members.

OECD PUBLISHING, 2, rue André-Pascal, 75775 PARIS CEDEX 16
(04 2018 18 1 P) ISBN 978-92-64-30968-5 – 2018

www.ingramcontent.com/pod-product-compliance
Lightning Source LLC
LaVergne TN
LVHW081408110826
845149LV00010B/1673
* 9 7 8 9 2 6 4 3 0 9 6 8 5 *